Praying Together

Randy Petersen

Publications International, Ltd.

Randy Petersen is the author of *Why Me, God?*, *Path to Heaven,* and
The Powerful Prayer of Jabez and coauthor of *God's Answers to Tough Questions*.
He earned a B.A. in ancient languages from Wheaton College before becoming
executive editor of *Bible Newsletter* and other publications. Now a full-time
freelance writer and editor, he has also contributed to more than 20 other
books, such as *The Revell Bible Dictionary* and *The Christian Book of Lists,* and
to a wide variety of magazines, including *Christian History*.

Louis Weber, CEO
Publications International, Ltd.
7373 North Cicero Avenue
Lincolnwood, Illinois 60712

ISBN-13: 978-1-4127-1018-3
ISBN-10: 1-4127-1018-9

Manufactured in U.S.A.

8 7 6 5 4 3 2 1

Contents

Why Pray Together?

~~~

*T*he power that comes from praying together isn't just a theory. It has been borne out in the lives of God's people throughout history. And every day there are more exciting instances of miraculous answers to these prayers. Churches are growing stronger through group prayer, and individuals are overcoming obstacles by praying with others.

It's happening all around you, but how can you make it happen in your own prayer life? By joining with others—a few or an entire congregation—and allowing God to work with and through your prayers.

In an era when waiting seven minutes for your microwave dinner to warm up seems like an eternity, praying with others may seem inconvenient. Waiting for answers might exhaust your patience. But that's because you haven't committed to it. When two hearts are praying as one, or when 200 hearts are praying as one, time becomes inconsequential, and the Holy Spirit dwells among you. Prayer becomes a precious event, not an ongoing list of personal wishes.

In this book you will see what has been done through group prayer and what can be done through praying together. After Jesus returned to his Father, a ragtag group of his followers joined together in prayer, just as he had told them to do. If you read through the Book of Acts you will see how this unlikely bunch summoned the power of God and changed the world. Their impact is felt today. The early church grew strong through prayer and so can you.

Jesus promised to be present whenever "two or three" gather in his name. Remember that promise as you meet in prayer with your spouse, your neighbors, your Bible study, or your church. Then be prepared to watch your faith grow as you experience the power of God in your prayer life.

The Mystery of Prayer

❧ ❧ ❧

Why God Wants Us to Talk with Him

The building shook.

That's what the Bible tells us about the first Christian prayer meeting on record. The early church gathered to pray, and "the place in which they were gathered together was shaken" (Acts 4:31). Were they at the epicenter of a minor earthquake, or were the people reeling from the emotional impact of their prayers? It doesn't really matter. The important thing is that those believers experienced the power of praying together.

In various ways, that power has been felt by millions of Christians throughout the ages. Many prayer groups have seen miraculous answers to their pleas. Some churches have bonded together by praying for particular needs. And countless families have learned that those who pray together stay together. Prayer has power, and the power seems to intensify when there are multiple people praying.

What is this force found in shared prayer? How does it work? What can it accomplish? And how can you tap into it?

This book will answer those questions and more. But if you're seeking a magic formula, some secret method of using group prayer to win success and riches, look elsewhere. When two or three or a thousand believers join together in prayer, they can indeed access supernatural power, but it's not for sale. People keep hunting for a way to harness divine forces to get what *they* want, but Christian prayer focuses on what *God* wants. The power of prayer resides in a vital relationship with the living God, a God who often surprises us with his answers, unleashing his dynamic love in ways we can't predict.

❦ ❦ ❦

Finding Emily

Scott and Vickie had a beautiful daughter, and they wanted another one. It seemed that adoption would be necessary, and they felt God leading them to adopt a child from Asia. Various agencies were helping American families adopt children from China, Vietnam, and elsewhere, and it involved a lot of paperwork. But Scott and Vickie put their names on a list and paid a fee...and they waited. And waited.

Every Thursday morning, Scott met with a men's Bible study group at his church. He was a bit shy about asking for prayer—surely other people had much greater needs—but eventually he told the group about the adoption situation, and they prayed. Every Thursday evening, Vickie met with a women's Bible study group, and they were praying too. Week after week, month after month, those groups kept praying that God would make the right things happen.

Eventually, Scott and Vickie were promised a particular six-month-old baby from China. They just had to make the final arrangements. It looked as if this long process was finally coming to a happy conclusion.

Then the whole thing fell apart. The adoption program closed, leaving many couples sorely disappointed. It reopened a year later, but much of the paperwork was overlooked in all the confusion. Still fueled by prayer, Scott and Vickie switched to another agency, one that quickly assigned them a child in Vietnam.

Full of praise and thanks, the prayer groups threw them a baby shower. But there were more trials ahead.

Their trip to pick up the child was postponed. Other adoptive parents were having trouble with this agency, and they discovered that it was grossly mismanaged. One staff member even absconded with some of the money Scott and Vickie had paid, so they had to come up with more money. They were giving up hope of ever getting this child.

By now the whole church was praying for them, and in July they received word of a newborn they could adopt. They quickly made travel plans, and on the last day of August they were standing in a government building in Vietnam waiting for the adoption ceremony to commence. They had waited two years, what was another hour? Finally an attorney entered with their infant, and the official adoption took place. Scott and Vickie had a few moments with the birth mother; they tried to ask about the care and feeding of the little girl, but there were no translators at hand, and the language barrier caused a lot of confusion. The mother frantically wrote them a note before she was ushered out of the room. The next morning, they managed to get the note translated. When they did, many things became clear.

In the note, the mother said she was a Christian, and she had been asking God to send someone to adopt her baby.

All of the confusion, the disappointments, the false starts, the lost money, the mismanagement—in a strange way, it all made sense now. Maybe all of it was God's way of adjusting the timing so that *this* child would get *these* parents. On both sides of the world, Christians were praying that God would guide this situation, and he certainly did. Though it had often seemed as if God had forgotten those prayers, he was actively answering them, according to his own timing. When all was said and done, Scott and Vickie felt convinced that God had chosen Emily just for them and guided the entire process to bring them together.

Prayer is a powerful thing, for God has bound and tied himself to it. No one can believe how powerful prayer is, and what it can do, except those who have learned it by experience.

—Martin Luther

What Is Prayer?

What is prayer? Many people think only about prayer *requests*. We pray *for* things, and God answers by giving us those things. When we talk about the power of prayer, most people assume we mean the power to get what we ask for. There are many stories like that of Scott and Vickie, in which miraculous answers to prayer testify to God's great power and love. But that's not the whole story. Prayer is much, much more than just requesting, and as we pray God reveals his power in various ways.

Reading through Scripture and thinking over two millennia of Christian experience, we see many aspects of prayer. Besides requests, it involves praise, thanksgiving, confession, celebration, and meditation. Prayers may be offered in front of congregations numbering in the thousands, within families of four or five, or in a single human heart. You may kneel to pray, or stand, or lie prostrate. You may shout praises or whisper apologies. You may pray as you drive, or as you work, or in the midst of an important conversation as you wonder what to say next.

Prayer has countless forms, but let's drill into its essence. How do we combine all of these activities into one definition? Well, we might say that, at heart, prayer is simply *hanging out with God*. That might sound a bit too casual to you, but it describes the basic relationship in which the various forms of prayer take place. Like "hanging out," prayer usually involves conversation, both speaking and listening, but it doesn't have to. Even when we don't know what words to use the Spirit of God still accepts our inner feelings (Romans 8:26). The crucial thing is that we are spending time with him.

We can learn a lot about prayer by comparing it to our human relationships. How do you interact with your best friend? How does a child converse with a parent? How would you act in the presence of a king, a president, or a celebrity you adore? All of these human exchanges can teach us about prayer, because in one way or another, God is like all of these.

He's a best friend. God knows us like no one else does, and he loves us with an amazing steadfastness. He is there for us. With your best friend, there are times you don't need to talk; you just enjoy each other's company. Or maybe you chat about the events of the day. You share your feelings and fears and struggles and smiles. It's the same with God.

You might say complimentary things to your best friend, or if you haven't returned a phone message for three days, you might apologize. Your friend might challenge you to do your best at some project or teach you how to do it better. You might ask your friend to do you a favor, and then give thanks after it's done. All of these are also elements of prayer: praise, confession, commitment, instruction, requests, and thanksgiving.

He's a parent. Of course God isn't just a friend. The Bible describes him as "our Father in heaven" and frequently refers to God's maternal compassion for people. This adds another dimension to the relationship. A child and a parent can have meaningful heart-to-heart conversations, but there is

a recognition that one has authority over the other.
The parent has the responsibility to care for the
child, to instruct and admonish when necessary.
Children, on the other hand, ask for things. Some
parents might complain that their kids are *always*
asking for things, but that's a crucial part of their
role in the relationship. They can't drive to the store
and shell out big bucks for a state-of-the-art
computer. Only the parents have the authority (and
money, and car) to do that, and the children must
rely on the parents' good graces.

So don't be shy about asking God for things. That's
part of your role in this relationship.

God is also the king of the universe, and our
interaction with him should reflect this reality as
well. Many of us don't really know how to relate to a
king, so we might think in terms of the president or
even a Hollywood celebrity. What would you do in a
meeting with such a person? If you're invited to
speak, you might blurt out some compliments. "I've
seen all your movies. You're the greatest." On your
best behavior, you would show great respect.

Of course that is true of God as well. We owe him far more respect than we'd offer a human celebrity. He enjoys hearing our praises, and he wants us to remember that our requests are always subject to his plans for us. It's good to ask for things, but don't treat him like a heavenly butler. And if you're disappointed with something he's done, you can share your honest feelings with him, but keep in mind that he's God and you're not.

There's a balance here, between the casual "hanging out" of best friends and the respectful adoration owed to our Creator. Occasionally a Christian writer will complain that people have been getting too chummy with God in recent years, and we need to restore a sense of awe to our faith. Maybe, but the Bible rarely tells people that they're too casual with God. The bigger danger comes from keeping him at arm's length—saying pious words without giving him your heart (Isaiah 29:13). God longs for a friendship with us, so we're really not pleasing him if we reject that kind of intimacy in the name of piety.

Every so often on a TV talk show, you'll see a gorgeous actor complaining that no one asks her out on dates anymore. That's usually hard to believe, but assuming it's true, think about what's going on there: Millions of people worship her, but she just wants someone to befriend her. Maybe God feels the same way. The praises are great, but he also wants us to share our hearts with him. He just wants to hang out with us.

Prayer is all of these things and more. Praising, pleading, promising, listening, learning, longing, confessing, complaining, and comparing notes. It's a multifaceted communication with a multifaceted God—as we see in the prayer the early Christians were praying when the building shook.

≈≈≈

Lord, ... grant to your servants to speak your word with all boldness, while you stretch out your hand to heal, and signs and wonders are performed through the name of your holy servant Jesus.

—*Acts 4:29–30*

❦ ❦ ❦

Shaken and Stirred

Why was all that shaking going on? What were those first-century Christians praying about? How did they make the building shudder? And what can we learn from them?

It all started a day earlier, when Peter and John passed a lame beggar on the way to the temple. Outside one of the temple gates, this man called out to them for money. They gave him something better. "In the name of Jesus Christ of Nazareth, stand up and walk" (Acts 3:6).

When he actually did, the two apostles might have been as surprised as anyone. Miracles had always been on the menu when Jesus was around, but he had returned to heaven a few weeks before this incident. Now a crowd was gathering around Peter and John, wondering how on earth they had given the beggar new legs. "Why do you stare at us," Peter protested, "as though by our own power or piety we had made him walk?" It was the name of Jesus that provided the power, he explained. They began to preach about the life-healing that could be found in Jesus.

Until they got arrested.

These might have been the same guards who had shown up in the Garden of Gethsemane a few months earlier, just as Jesus was crying out, "Your will be done!" On that occasion, Peter had pulled a sword and hacked off someone's ear. This time he went quietly. He and John spent the night in jail.

There were 5,000 followers of Christ in Jerusalem at that point, and we know they were gathering regularly in small groups to pray. The Book of Acts tells us that they met "from house to house" for fellowship, bread-breaking, teaching, and prayer (Acts 2:42, 46 KJV). No doubt, while Peter and John languished behind bars, these prayer groups around the city were calling for God's protection. The two former fishermen faced the official council the next morning—the same rulers who had condemned

Christ to death. *What gives you the right to do this?* the council demanded. That just gave Peter another chance to preach about Jesus.

Apparently, his message wasn't brilliant. It was obvious that they were "unschooled, ordinary men," but the council "took note that these men had been with Jesus" (Acts 4:13 NIV). For the past three years Jesus had been on the council's agenda, until the fateful wee-hours meeting at which they had finally dealt with the problem once and for all—or so they thought. The Crucifixion was supposed to put an end to the threat of Jesus. But now they were viewing two of his followers, common laborers who preached like Jesus, healed like Jesus, and stood up before them with courage, just like Jesus. And what could they charge them with? Fraud? Claiming power they didn't have? That might have worked . . . until someone pointed out the lame beggar—the man they had all passed a thousand times on the way to work—standing in the back of the room. Yes, *standing*.

Peter and John were released with merely a stern warning: *Don't do any more preaching!* They explained that it was really up to God whether they preached anymore. In spite of their insolence, they were set free. Was it the power of prayer that limited the council to this judicial slap on the wrist? Was it the cumulative force of the requests rising from the Christian prayer groups newly formed throughout the city?

We only know that Peter and John returned to "their own people"—probably the house church they were part of—and told them what had happened. In response, the people prayed. They praised God for his creation. They quoted Scripture back to him. They told God what was happening. And they asked God to grant them boldness and continue to work miracles through them.

And after they prayed, the place shook. But that wasn't the only expression of power. "They were all filled with the Holy Spirit and spoke the word of God with boldness" (Acts 4:31). Prayer didn't just shake their world—it shook *them*.

~ ~ ~

Call to me and I will answer you, and
will tell you great and hidden things
that you have not known.

—*Jeremiah 33:3*

~ ~ ~

Magic Words

Where does the power of prayer come from? All
sorts of religions and mythologies through the ages
have looked for power in "magic words."
"Abracadabra," says the sultan, and the genie pops
out of the bottle, granting three wishes. Others offer
incantations, trusting that specific utterances will
conjure up divine power. Even some Christians have
bought into that general idea, believing that the tag
line "in Jesus' name" is required for a prayer to be
answered.

Jesus spoke specifically against this idea of magic
words in his Sermon on the Mount. The Gentiles—
those who didn't know the true God—just babbled

on, heaping up empty phrases, thinking that they could manipulate God if they said enough prayers. "Do not be like them," Jesus said, and introduced a radical new kind of prayer. "Father in heaven, hallowed be your name..." (Matthew 6:7–13).

It is a sad irony that many Christians babble through the Lord's Prayer without thinking, as if the mere utterance of the words would win points with God—when this is precisely the approach Jesus criticized *immediately before he gave us this prayer*. The power of the Lord's Prayer—or any prayer—comes from its recipient. It's not how often you say it, or how accurately you recite it but the fact that you're connecting with your heavenly Father. *He's* got the power, not us, and he is beyond our manipulation. We cannot force his hand. In fact, the power of prayer comes from the opposite approach, not trying to control him, but giving him

> Before they call
> I will answer,
> while they are yet
> speaking I will hear.
> —*Isaiah 65:24*

control, acknowledging him as wise and holy, asking that his kingdom be advanced in this world, wanting his will to be done.

Babbling does no good, Jesus said, because "your Father knows what you need before you ask him" (Matthew 6:8). That raises a good question: Why then should we pray at all? If God already knows our needs, we shouldn't have to pray, should we? If we're just going to pray "Thy will be done"—well, isn't God going to do what he wants anyway?

~ ~ ~

Why Pray?

Are we disturbing God by requesting things? Hardly. The Bible urges, "Let your requests be made known to God" (Philippians 4:6). In fact, Jesus told a story about a woman who nagged an unjust judge to hear her case until he relented. If even a bad judge gives in like that, Jesus concluded, "will not God grant justice to his chosen ones who cry to him day and night?" (Luke 18:7).

God wants us to ask for things. Why? Especially when he knows our needs better than we do, what's the point?

Jesus compared our prayers to the requests a child would make of a parent. "Is there anyone among you who, if your child asks for bread, will give a stone?" (Matthew 7:9). Let's look a bit deeper into that parent-child comparison. When a child is very young, the parents meet its needs—food, clothing, shelter. Parents hear a baby's cries and interpret them as requests for changing, feeding, or cuddling. As time goes on, the child develops the ability to articulate desires. The parent is still assessing needs and meeting them, but there's a new factor involved: what the child wants. These desires aren't always best for the child, and wise parents often say no. If your son asks for candy at dinnertime, will you give him broccoli? Well, yes, if you're a good parent. In the same way, God often hears our requests and gives us something different, something that's better for us.

Sometimes, however, parents give a child exactly what's requested. What brand of sneakers do you want? What color shall we paint your room? What toppings do you want on your pizza? Wise parents give their children choices, so the kids will develop good decision-making abilities. That's part of growing up. As children develop their own tastes, their own abilities, their own interests, parents get to know them better. The parent-child relationship is deepened.

Imagine a situation where a parent makes every decision for a child—what to eat, what to wear, what to do for fun—even when that child is a teenager! That sort of control is essential during infancy, but a child develops individuality through the years. He or she becomes a distinct person, not just a robot programmed by the parents. Good parents recognize the personal preferences of their children, and they come to accept and enjoy their individuality.

The same is true with God. He doesn't give us everything we want, but he *cares* about what we want. He cares about the unique desires and interests that make us who we are.

Let's consider another parent-child moment. A teenager reaches out to Mom or Dad and says, "I need your advice." How do Mom and Dad feel at that point?

Needed!

Now maybe they would have offered advice anyway, but it's great to be asked. And what is that teenager saying when she asks for advice? "You have wisdom beyond my own. I'm unable to deal with this by myself. I need your help. I trust you to give the advice that will truly help me." What parent wouldn't feel appreciated?

For the same reason, God loves it when we seek his help. Every request is an offering of praise, because we acknowledge that God has the power to meet our needs. Every request is an expression of trust, because we rely on him to do what we can't.

Why pray? Well, as we have seen, prayer is not just about requesting things. Those who don't know God might babble their magic words in an effort to make

God fulfill their wishes. But Jesus taught us a new way to pray, coming before God as "our Father," committing ourselves to work for his kingdom and to do what he wants. Prayer is quality time spent with our Creator. We share our desires, but we also learn his.

So the power of prayer is not just a matter of getting our purchase orders fulfilled. God often grants our requests, and sometimes he amazes us with the way he shakes our world. But he also shakes *us*. He forgives and delivers us, empowers and emboldens us. When you talk about the power of prayer, never forget about his power at work within you.

~ ~ ~

Lord, teach us to pray. We want to feel that earthshaking power, but most of all, we want to draw closer to you. Merge our requests with your desires to do amazing things in and through us. This we humbly pray in your holy name. Amen.

~ ~ ~

The Strange Power of "Two or Three"

~~~

Where Jesus Brings His Special Presence

*W*hen last we left the apostle Peter, the room was shaking. He and John, free from prison, had reported back to their prayer group, which offered up some praises that nearly brought down the house, literally.

Ten years later, Peter was back in the slammer. Cracking down on this new Christian movement, King Herod had already killed James, who was John's brother and Peter's fishing buddy. Now he had Peter in custody and was just waiting for the right time to execute him.

The night before his scheduled trial, the authorities were taking no chances, chaining Peter to two guards, with other guards outside the door. As they knew, this whole Christian business had start when the disciples swiped a body from a guarded tomb. They weren't about to let them stage a jailbreak.

Meanwhile, there was a late-night prayer meeting going on at the home of Mary. (This was one of several Marys of the New Testament—not Jesus' mother, not Magdalene, not Martha's sister. This Mary was Mark's mother.) You can imagine the risk involved in such a meeting, when leaders were being arrested and killed, but many still gathered there to pray. Dire hours required higher power.

We don't know what they prayed for. Did they pray for Peter's release? Did they pray for God's name to be glorified, no matter what happened to Peter? From the earthshaking model in Acts 4, we can guess that they praised God, briefed him on the situation, and challenged him to act with miraculous power. That prayer was certainly answered.

That night, Peter awoke to a jab in his side. His prison cell was filled with light. "Get up!" someone said. The chains fell off Peter's wrists. "Put your clothes on and follow me!" the voice ordered. It seemed to be an angel leading him to safety. It also seemed to be a dream.

Iron gates were opening for them as they walked out of the prison. There were no guards stopping them. If they were there, they were sleeping. Then the angel left, and Peter found himself on the street outside the prison, slowly adjusting to the reality of his situation. He made his way down the road to Mary's house, where he probably assumed people would be praying for him.

Many homes in that day were built with rooms around a central courtyard and a gate securing the front entrance. The prayer meeting was no doubt going on in an inner room, perhaps a second-story room, when Peter knocked at the gate. A maid named Rhoda came out to answer it.

"It's me. Peter."

This was amazing. Rhoda had just been praying for Peter's release and here he was, knocking at the gate.

Overjoyed, she ran in to tell the others. One problem: She forgot to open the gate.

"You'll never guess who's here," she told the others. "It's Peter!"

"You're out of your mind," they protested.

Meanwhile, Peter continued to knock at the gate, and eventually they let him in. He described his miraculous release and told them to spread the word.

> Rejoice always, pray without ceasing, give thanks in all circumstances; for this is the will of God in Christ Jesus for you.
> —1 Thessalonians 5:16–18

From the start, the Christian church relied on prayer. This was their link to the mighty power of God, a power that kept amazing them. It wasn't that they were especially good at praying. It wasn't even the amount of faith they had—as we see in their incredulous response to Peter at the gate. It was merely that they prayed, inviting God to work his will in the circumstances of their lives.

➳➳➳

Help Wanted

Lynn needed a job. She had left a corporate position to tend to family needs, but after a year and a half she was ready to resume climbing the ladder. Though she sent her resume to dozens of firms, seeking an administrative position, few were interested. Only one job prospect got as far as an interview. That was for a high-level position with a generous salary. Lynn worried that the job might be too demanding, that it might take her away from her family, but how could she pass it up if it was offered? Before and after the interview, she prayed, "God, help me get this job." She didn't.

As time went on, Lynn was getting more and more frantic. Her savings were nearly depleted. How much longer could her unemployment last? Of course there was also the emotional weight of worry and rejection. Corporate America didn't want her. As far as they were concerned, Lynn had nothing to offer. That's hard for anyone to take.

One afternoon Lynn expressed these feelings to her friend Sandy, who suggested that they pray together about it. Now, prayer was not a foreign concept for Lynn. She had been launching many desperate pleas toward the Almighty. But this was something different, a meeting of the hearts, a side-by-side stroll up to the throne of God.

Sandy took Lynn's hand and both women bowed their heads. "Lord, we ask that you find Lynn the perfect job for her," Sandy prayed. She went on, detailing the needs Lynn had just been talking about—both financial and emotional—and asking God to meet each one.

Lynn tilted her head toward heaven and told God she would take *anything*.

This became a matter of prayer for several women in the church, and before long one of them spied an ad in the paper. The job was an odd one, she thought, but it just might fit Lynn. She passed it on, and Lynn agreed that it didn't match her planned career path, but she had told God she would take anything. So she answered the ad, interviewed, and took the job as cook and housekeeper for a monastery.

Now, several months into her new responsibilities, Lynn considers it the "perfect job" for her. Great people. Great benefits. A reasonable schedule. And a way to use both her creative and administrative skills for a good cause. She looks back to that moment when Sandy grabbed her hand. That was the turning point. Their prayers were beautifully answered.

What kind of divine power was sparked in that moment? Did that mutual prayer have more oomph than Lynn's personal requests? Would Lynn have gotten that job if she had never prayed with Sandy? It's hard to deal with hypothetical questions. Maybe Lynn would have gotten that job anyway, but maybe not. We're tempted to look for some kind of magic spark ignited when two Christians bow their heads, and maybe that exists, but let's pull back and look at the more obvious elements of the situation.

Lynn had been looking in the wrong direction, assuming that her career would pick up where it left off, in the corporate world. As she saw it, she needed a high-powered job, and she was frustrated because she couldn't find one.

Sandy began praying about all of Lynn's needs—not just the need for a paycheck. And somehow that emphasis got Lynn to the point of enlarging her own vision. She would take what the Lord provided.

That mutual prayer with Sandy also grew into a network of prayer support. Several women began to pray for Lynn and pay attention to her needs. So when one of them noticed a want ad, she thought of Lynn and passed it on.

But isn't that just networking? Wouldn't that have happened if Lynn had just told a few friends to keep an eye out for job possibilities? No, probably not. They would have been looking for jobs in the corporate world. It was the attitude of prayer that got them all to open up to new possibilities. And that led to Lynn's "perfect job" in a monastery.

❧ ❧ ❧

O Lord, support us all the day long, until the shadows lengthen and the evening comes, and the busy world is hushed. Then in Thy mercy grant us a safe lodging, and a holy rest, and peace at the last.

—*Book of Common Prayer*

❧ ❧ ❧

How Do Groups Help Us?

Much of the power of praying together comes from obvious sources. We saw how Scott and Vickie gained emotional support from their prayer groups. This empowered them to continue their efforts to adopt, even when it became very frustrating. The Bible says, "Rejoice with those who rejoice, weep with those who weep" (Romans 12:15), and these groups did exactly that. Lynn experienced the same emotional support from her group of praying friends. In many cases, such support enables us to answer our own prayers, in a way. We pray, "Thy will be done," and God certainly wants us to participate in the answering of that prayer by *doing* his will. The emotional support of other believers can help us do that. As it says in Hebrews, "Let us consider how to provoke one another to love and good deeds" (Hebrews 10:24).

Groups can also provide perspective, guidance, and a broader wisdom. We saw how Sandy's prayer opened Lynn's mind to new possibilities. And certainly, if Scott and Vickie were crazy to pursue their adoption, the good friends in their prayer groups would have told them so.

Try driving with one eye—but not for long. Even if the vision in that eye is 20/20, you won't have depth perception. You need input from a second eye in order to get the whole picture. It's the same way with prayer groups. One member of a prayer group might ask the others to pray that she would be able to patch up a rocky relationship with her boyfriend. But maybe the others realize that the boyfriend is all wrong for her. As they voice their prayers for wholeness and guidance and God-honoring love, she might get the picture that a breakup might be the best answer to her prayer. Or, after the final Amen, a good friend might tell her that directly. In any case, the additional input of a prayer group gives us perspective, so we can pray for the proper things.

Jesus said, "If two of you agree on earth about anything you ask, it will be done for you by my Father in heaven" (Matthew 18:19). We must always be careful about those scriptural "blank checks." He's not saying you should buy a lottery ticket with your pals and pray to win. But if there are two or three believers agreeing on something to pray for, there is already a mix of God-given wisdom.

Long before networking became a hot topic in the business world, the church was practicing it. The New Testament teaches that Christians have different spiritual gifts, which fit together for the growth of the church and the glory of God. The church is described as the "body of Christ," with different members functioning as eyes, ears, hands, feet, and so on. The body of Christ does the work of Christ, as different members use their unique abilities. And so, not only can you be the answer to your own prayers, on occasion, but maybe you can answer someone else's, or they can answer yours. When the entire church, or even just a prayer group, is committed to the principle of "God's will be done," we will find ourselves answering one another's prayers, whether we realize it or not.

And so a friend sees a want ad and passes it on. Someone in your prayer group hears you praying about your car troubles and volunteers her expertise in auto mechanics. A prayer partner recognizes your emotional stress and recommends a good counselor. Maybe you've seen this sort of networking happen among the people you pray with. God uses these connections to accomplish his will.

Support, perspective, networking—these are a few of the natural ways groups can help us. But let's not forget the supernatural element. There is still some kind of power in group prayer that we can't explain.

~~~

See, I am the Lord, the God of all flesh;
is anything too hard for me?
—*Jeremiah 32:27*

❧ ❧ ❧

A Miracle of Birth

Bill and Ardythe were eagerly awaiting the birth of their first child, but there were major complications. Ardythe was in labor for 36 hours, growing weaker every minute. Her own mother had died in childbirth while bearing her, and Ardythe had experienced some major health problems growing up. So it wasn't unthinkable that this happy occasion could turn tragic.

Finally the doctors performed a Caesarean section and the baby was born, but there was a problem with his lungs. Mucus was collecting there, and the child wasn't breathing properly. With Ardythe's weakened state, the doctors were saying it didn't look good for either mother or son. Bill braced himself for a double loss.

The church that Bill and Ardythe attended was hosting a missionary conference that week, with meetings every night. A nurse who went to that church told the pastor about the crisis, and he mentioned it to the guest speaker. They stopped the meeting and offered up prayers for mother and child.

As it happened, the next morning a machine was delivered to the hospital, a machine that had recently been invented to clear mucus out of the lungs of newborns. It was just what the baby needed. The child rapidly returned to health, as did Ardythe. Bill was breathing easier, too. And an entire church had a greater appreciation for the power of praying together.

≈ ≈ ≈

There is nothing that makes us love a man so much as praying for him; and when you can once do this sincerely, you have fitted your soul for the performance of everything that is kind and civil towards him.

—*William Law*, Serious Call

Two or Three

Where is Jesus? Try that as a discussion question around the dinner table sometime. There are several possible answers, all quite correct. Jesus stands *at the right hand of God.* You might also say he is *everywhere,* sharing the divine trait of omnipresence. And through the Holy Spirit, Jesus lives *in the heart of every believer.*

> I will extol you, my God and King, and bless your name forever and ever. Every day I will bless you, and praise your name forever and ever. Great is the Lord, and greatly to be praised; his greatness is unsearchable.
> —Psalm 145:1–3

But there's another answer we need to pay special attention to. It's found in Matthew 18:20, as Jesus says, "Where two or three are gathered in my name, I am there among them."

Jesus exists in a special way wherever Christians gather in his name. This fact gives us the notion that there is a special power in group prayer. It doesn't mean that individual prayer is any less effective or important. But Jesus is *specially* present when Sandy grabs Lynn's hand to pray or when a missionary conference comes to a halt so a church can pray for a newborn baby. When a prayer group brings a request before the Lord, Jesus is with them.

～～～

In His Name

Have you noticed the phrase that appears in Jesus' promise: "In my name"? He is specially present when we gather *in his name*. What is Jesus talking about? What does it mean to gather in Jesus' name? Or to pray in his name?

Consider the case of Tim and Barb, who were given tickets to a major football game. Their neighbor

John was the giver, a season ticket holder who had to be away on business that weekend. He said they were great seats.

The whole experience was far better than they could have imagined. When Tim and Barb drove to the game, John's parking pass got them a free space close to the stadium. When they showed their tickets, they were directed up to a luxury box. "Oh, you must be John's friends," said the hostess. "We'll take care of you." They had a great view of the game, plus all sorts of food and beverages. Whatever they wanted, John had arranged that it would be put on his tab. They enjoyed this experience "in John's name."

That's a very accurate picture of our standing with God. Jesus pays our way. The New Testament makes it clear that we can't earn God's favor on our own; we must trust in the sacrifice of Christ. And so we approach the throne of the Father, and he says, "Oh, you must be friends of my son, Jesus."

Let's look at a different picture. Say your friend Sam Jones is getting married, and you're invited to a swanky hotel for the reception. You enter the hotel and what do you say? "I'm with the Sam Jones party." You are gathering with others in the name of Sam Jones.

In a very real way, a Christian worship service is the wedding reception of Jesus Christ and his bride, the church. We gather in his name—because of him, to meet with him, to please him, to celebrate him.

But there's even more to this idea. We bear the name of Jesus. We are Christians—little Christs. The Bible calls us members of the family, Jesus' brothers and sisters. Parents might tell their children, "Be careful how you act out there, in the neighborhood and at school, because you carry the family name. Anything you do reflects on us, on all of us, because we share the same name."

Not only do we bear the name of Jesus; we also share his mission. We are now engaged in seeking his kingdom, spreading his redemption, sharing his love. We not only carry the name, we act in it.

One young writer had a phobia about phone calls. He hated to call people for interviews, because he always worried that he was interrupting something more important. Then he got an assignment from a major magazine that involved calling 30 leading executives and asking about trends in their business. He was dreading it . . . until he started doing it. Then he found that the name of the magazine gave him some authority. He simply gave his name and identified the magazine he was working for, and these leaders opened up to him. They were eager to be quoted in his article. And so the writer easily made all 30 calls and then some. What made the difference? He was working "in the name of" that magazine.

All of this gives us some context for some of the big promises of Jesus. He said, for instance, "If in my name you ask me for anything, I will do it" (John 14:14). But does it really work like that?

From the beginning of sophomore year through the end of high school, Jimmy prayed that Janet, a classmate with a cute smile and a Southern drawl, would fall in love with him. Every day he prayed, being sure to say, "In Jesus' name," at the end of each prayer. It never happened. Did Jesus renege on his promise?

No, because prayer is more than an order form. You can't just put Jesus' credit card number at the bottom and expect the merchandise to arrive. Prayer is a relationship. We gather in Jesus' name to honor him. We come before the Father in Jesus' name because of his sacrifice. We live our lives bearing Jesus' name because we're part of the family. And we work in Jesus' name, doing Jesus' work, for Jesus' purposes. So when we pray in Jesus' name, it comes out of this whole experience. We want what he wants. We live for him, and so we should be asking for the sorts of things that help us do better at living and working in his name.

"You ask and do not receive," James says, "because you ask wrongly, in order to spend what you get on your pleasures" (James 4:3). We don't need to scold Jimmy for asking "wrongly," but we need to encourage his faith to grow. It's not about your pleasure, Jimmy. It's about his name. So open your eyes, and see all the things you can do and be—in the marvelous name of Jesus.

≈ ≈ ≈

When Three Become Four

In a prayer group, somebody could say that to Jimmy. Where two or three are gathered in the name of Jesus, there is a continual reminder of what it means to exist in his name. We talk about our needs, our issues, our personal dramas, and the group listens like Jesus, comforts like Jesus, or offers the kind of challenges that fill the gospels. Playing Christ for one another, we help one another become more Christlike.

There's a curious story in the Old Testament book of Daniel. Three Jewish friends of the prophet Daniel refuse to bow down to the king's idol, and they are thrown into a blazing furnace. Then the king looks into the furnace and says, "Was it not three men that we threw bound into the fire? . . . But I see four men unbound, walking in the middle of the fire, and they are not hurt; and the fourth has the appearance of a god" (Daniel 3:24–25).

In the original Aramaic, the last line reads, "...the fourth looks like a son of the gods," which makes us wonder if Jesus made an early appearance in that furnace, comforting and protecting these men who were loyal to God's name. In any case, it's a picture of what happens when Christians pray. No matter what kind of struggles you're facing, even when your life feels like a blazing furnace, wherever two or three of us gather in his name, there's a fourth one standing with us in the fire.

～～～

Lord, thank you for standing with us in the flames of life. We sense your presence as we pray together. Fill us with your love. Push us to follow you more closely. Inspire us to do great things in your name. Amen.

～～～

Body Building

How the Church Grows Through Prayer

It was a new church, meeting every Sunday in a high school auditorium. The founders had made it a point to invite people who didn't have much Christian background. Basic doctrines were thoroughly explained. The bulletin listed not just the reference of the weekly Scripture reading, but also the page number of that text in the Bibles that were made available as people entered. It couldn't be assumed that these churchgoers knew how to find Malachi or Matthew, or even that they owned a Bible of their own.

By its fourth year, this congregation numbered around 300, and many of these were new believers who had begun a relationship with Christ through the exciting, accepting ministry of this church.

Then Marilyn got sick. Besides her duties at the helm of the thriving music program of the church, she was also the pastor's wife. The day before they left on their summer vacation, Marilyn received a stunning diagnosis—she had Hodgkins disease, cancer of the lymph nodes. In the following months, Marilyn underwent an aggressive regimen of chemotherapy, but she continued as music director.

In one of those "spiritual gift" tests, Marilyn had determined that she had the gift of faith. Well, she needed it. Round after round of chemotherapy weakened her, but she kept a cheery attitude. The church was praying for her. Other churches were praying for her. People around the country would call to ask, "How's Marilyn?" And the answer was usually positive. She seemed to be beating this thing.

Until December, when she began to run a very high fever. In the midst of her fifth round of chemo, she basically had no immune system left. Though she was quickly put on antibiotics, she just got worse.

Three days before Christmas, Marilyn went into the hospital. Doctors gave her antibiotics intravenously, but that seemed to do no good. They had no answers for this new mystery disease. X-rays and blood tests failed to tell them what the problem was, so they took her off all medication and sent her home for the holiday.

With his wife ailing at home, the pastor conducted the Christmas Eve service as usual, but he seemed to be in a fog. The sturdy faith they both had shown through the whole ordeal was being pushed to its limit. The church had been exulting in Marilyn's successful fight against cancer, but now they were stunned to think that she might lose the battle.

Lauree was a church member who had known Marilyn for years, even before the new church began. When she called Marilyn the day after Christmas to wish her well, she was shocked and frightened by what she heard. "Marilyn could barely talk," Lauree said later, "and she sounded very worn down emotionally. At that point, Marilyn herself wasn't sure if she would get better."

On New Year's Eve, Marilyn went back to the hospital with a fever spiking past 106 degrees. Still baffled, doctors put her in intensive care, pumping eight powerful antibiotics through her weakened body. One physician told Marilyn's parents to prepare for the worst. There was one possible course of action, but it was risky. They could draw fluid from Marilyn's lungs, which might help them name the disease, but that required general anesthesia, and they weren't sure if Marilyn's body could bear the trauma. Yet there seemed to be no other choice.

They went ahead with the procedure on Monday morning, January 2, and Marilyn did come through it. But it might take another few days to get the results; could she hold on that long?

Lauree called the church office on Tuesday morning for an update. There were still no answers, and Marilyn's life was hanging in the balance. "I was scared and frustrated, and wished there was something I could do," said Lauree. She talked it over with her sister, and they decided to call an impromptu prayer meeting for that night at 7:30. They called a few church leaders to conduct the meeting, but most were out of town or had other commitments. They would have to make this happen themselves. So Lauree and her sister began making phone calls. Soon it became apparent that a living room wouldn't hold the number of people who said they'd come, so they arranged to use the chapel of the "parent church" of their congregation, the church Marilyn had grown up in.

By 7:30 the place was packed. People had to squeeze up onto the platform, and latecomers stood out in the hall. Unaccustomed to leading such a service, Lauree just followed the pattern used in church each Sunday: a few songs and Bible verses to start with. "Trust and Obey." "It Is Well with My Soul." Songs that Marilyn had always loved. And a reading from Romans 8: "If God is for us, who is against us?"

Then Lauree asked the people to pray. Anyone who wanted to pray out loud could do so. One by one, people stood, asking God to take special care of Marilyn. They asked for a miracle of healing. They asked that the doctors be given wisdom. They asked for strength and comfort for Marilyn's husband and children. They asked that, if it was God's will, he might keep Marilyn here on earth with all those who loved her.

Then Marilyn's mother-in-law arrived and announced that there was already an answer to their prayers. She had just received a phone call. The doctors had identified the illness as a rare strain of pneumonia, but it was treatable, with one of the eight antibiotics they were already giving Marilyn. She wasn't out of the woods yet, but they knew what they needed to do.

By the next morning, Marilyn's fever had broken, and she was speaking coherently for the first time in days. The doctors were amazed at how quickly her condition improved. They expected her to be in the ICU for a week and hospitalized for a week after that. In five days she was home. In the weeks that followed, her oncologist determined that the final round of chemotherapy was unnecessary. After some radiation treatment later that year, the cancer was in remission.

And now, a decade later, Marilyn is in fine health, continuing her work as music director in a church that's growing stronger all the time.

❦ ❦ ❦

Do not worry about anything, but in everything by prayer and supplication with thanksgiving let your requests be made known to God. And the peace of God, which surpasses all under-standing, will guard your hearts and your minds in Christ Jesus.

—*Philippians 4:6–7*

❦ ❦ ❦

The Real Miracle

There is no doubt in Lauree's mind that God worked a miracle in answer to the prayers voiced in that chapel. Marilyn and her family would agree. In fact, that meeting has become legendary in the history of that church.

But a closer analysis reveals that this isn't a perfect answer-to-prayer story. A skeptic might say that God's timing was a bit off. The doctors actually identified the mystery disease a short time *before* the prayer meeting started. And the antibiotic that would defeat that disease was already coursing through Marilyn's veins days earlier, as one of the eight desperately prescribed by the doctors. If you were writing this script, you would have all those things come *after* the prayer meeting, or even *simultaneous* with the prayer meeting. Why didn't it happen like that?

Maybe the healing wasn't the entire miracle.

Remember that a broad network of friends had already been praying for Marilyn for several months, and her recovery was remarkable, so there's no question: God was answering prayer in this situation. But consider some other aspects.

There's Lauree's story. Finding herself in a leadership vacuum, she stepped up and became a leader. Sure, she was terrified, but this was something God had asked her to do, and she did it. What a formative experience in her spiritual life!

This also becomes a tale of two churches. The two churches didn't have a lot in common—except their faith in Christ and their love for Marilyn and her family. These factors brought them together for this prayer meeting. And the fact that so many people from both churches showed up on short notice to pray—that was in itself a miracle.

The believers from the new church didn't know a lot about prayer. What an education this was for them! What did they learn by praying alongside the more experienced Christians of the parent church? Did those more experienced believers get a reminder of the power of simple faith?

And, if you're concerned about timing, could you imagine a better way to teach that God answers prayer? Instead of waiting a day or two for the results, the group hears that their prayers *are already being answered!*

In the Old Testament, people built altars or other monuments to remind them of God's miracles. After one battle in which God intervened to bring victory, Samuel set up a memorial he called *Ebenezer,* Hebrew for "Rock of Help," saying "Thus far the

Lord has helped us" (1 Samuel 7:12). Marilyn's miracle was an Ebenezer for her church, one of several along the way.

～～～

The military has a term for unanticipated results of their actions: *collateral damage.* They aim for a military target, but sometimes other people or buildings get hurt. We need to turn that notion completely around when we talk about answers to prayer. We might pray for one thing, but there are often "collateral blessings." Sometimes God answers prayers we don't even pray. Marilyn's miracle resulted in the strengthening of two churches, the education of new believers, and the development of new leadership. That's the sort of thing that happens when Christians pray together.

> If you abide in me, and my words abide in you, ask for whatever you wish, and it will be done for you.
> —John 15:7

❖ ❖ ❖

Priorities

People come to prayer with various needs and concerns. In a group situation, they share these needs with others and invite everyone to pray with them. That can result in some interesting combinations.

In one prayer circle, a member might say, "Well, I've been a little down lately. Maybe you could pray that I'll feel better."

That's a legitimate request. But the next person might say, "Our daughter just left home, and we don't know where she is. Could you pray that we'll find her?"

It's not that the second person is more important than the first, but the need is much more drastic. Prayer groups can pray for all these matters, from the seemingly trivial to the obviously critical, and they should. But the very act of presenting these requests to the Lord puts them in a new light.

And here's the collateral blessing. The depressed person might suddenly think, "Hey, my problems aren't all that bad compared to my friend here, who's worried sick over her daughter. I'm going to step out of my own doldrums and pray for her. I'm going to do all I can to help her." And that might be just what the doctor ordered.

Or consider a church that's engaged in a building project. A prayer group might be raising all sorts of concerns about money and mortgages, but then someone prays, "Lord, our desire is that this new building might welcome more people to come in and get to know you." And suddenly everyone remembers what it's all about.

In the presence of the Lord, we try to think with his mind, and that might change the way we see things. "Strive first for the kingdom of God and his righteousness," Jesus said, "and all these things will be given to you as well" (Matthew 6:33). He had just been telling his disciples not to worry about the basic necessities of life—food, drink, clothing. "All these things" would be provided, if they put God's kingdom first.

That same kind of prioritizing can occur as we pray.
There's nothing wrong with asking God for those
basic necessities—food on the table, this month's
rent, a better mood—but prayer puts us in the
kingdom's throne room, and we need to pay
attention to the things that will advance the cause of
the kingdom.

The dear God hears and pities all;
He knoweth all our wants;
And what we blindly ask of him
His love withholds or grants.

And so I sometimes think our prayers
Might well be merged in one,
And nest and perch and hearth and church
Repeat, "Thy will be done."
                                    —John Greenleaf Whittier

≈ ≈ ≈

Wisdom

Many cars these days come equipped with a GPS—Global Positioning System—that can tell you exactly where you are on earth. How does this work? Triangulation. This contraption beams a signal to three different satellites, measuring the distance. Every spot on earth can be defined by those three unique measurements. It takes information from all three sources to pin down your precise location. You might think of a prayer group as something like that.

Many individuals have wasted a lot of time praying for things they shouldn't have. God doesn't seem to mind. Even an errant prayer is a cry of faith. But think of the emotional energy invested in praying for unsatisfying jobs, unhealthy love affairs, or unnecessary windfalls of money. When you gather to pray with two or three (or more) other believers, you get a new perspective on what you really need. The "Divine Positioning System" does its triangulation to reveal where you are and where you need to go. Do you really want that job or that love affair or that money? How will it affect your faith? Will it advance God's kingdom in any way? Or in another year will you be praying for another job, another love affair, or more money? Wise prayer partners will ask those questions.

Or perhaps they will just voice those challenges in their prayers. "Lord, you know what's best for this person's heart. Provide a healthy relationship to meet those needs."

Of course there are busybodies in prayer groups who think they know what's best for everyone else. Be careful about this, or people will learn not to divulge anything personal in your group. Scripture speaks of such challenges made in a spirit of "gentleness," with an awareness of one's own temptations (Galatians 6:1). What we're talking about is the use of the spiritual gifts of the body of Christ. Some have a gift of wisdom, others have encouragement, others faith. You can use all of these gifts to help everyone pray better.

❈ ❈ ❈

Guidance

There's an interesting phrase that pops up in various forms in the New Testament: "It seemed good to the Holy Spirit, and to us" (Acts 15:28). The early church leaders met to figure out whether Gentiles could be invited into the church, and after prayer and debate, they used this phrase to report their decisions. Even now, there are many times when church groups meet to discuss a course of action, and then they bow to pray—and they come out of that prayer knowing what to do. It's not a thundering voice from heaven, but it just "seems good" to do this or that.

Jesus promised that the Holy Spirit would "guide you into all the truth" (John 16:13), and that's what happens. Half of any conversation is listening, and the same should be true of prayer. Individually, we can seek the Lord's guidance as we pray, and we can also do so in group settings.

❧ ❧ ❧

Unity

A church in Missouri was thinking about hiring a new youth pastor, but the congregation was split on the issue. Some believed the new hire would expand the ministry of the church; others thought they couldn't afford it. The issue was getting quite contentious, so several women who supported the hiring decided to get together and pray about it. Well, they really had their minds made up, so they were praying that the other side would see the light.

But a funny thing happened as they prayed. These women realized that they were telling God what to do, not asking what he wanted. In one hour of prayer, their attitude shifted completely. They came out of that meeting ready for whatever God wanted, willing to let him lead the way.

Presumably, there were similar prayer meetings among those on the other side, because when the congregation eventually voted, there was little rancor, just a healthy discussion, and 95 percent voted to hire the new youth pastor.

Similar stories could be told by many churches around the world. And on a much larger scale, we can look at the miraculously peaceful power shift in South Africa in the 1990s. Political observers predicted a bloodbath in that racially torn nation, but it didn't happen. What the headlines didn't report was that there were hundreds of prayer groups in South Africa meeting around the clock to pray for a peaceful transition.

Dealing with racially mixed churches that included both Jews and Gentiles, the apostle Paul begged each group to make "every effort to maintain the unity of the Spirit in the bond of peace. There is one body and one Spirit, just as you were called to the one hope of your calling, one Lord, one faith, one baptism, one God and Father of all, who is above all and through all and in all" (Ephesians 4:3–6). When we kneel beside one another in prayer, we begin to realize all we have in common.

≈ ≈ ≈

I pray that the God of our Lord Jesus
Christ, the Father of glory, may give
you a spirit of wisdom and revelation
as you come to know him, so that,
with the eyes of your heart
enlightened, you may know what is the
hope to which he has called you, what
are the riches of his glorious
inheritance among the saints, and what
is the immeasurable greatness of his
power for us who believe, according
to the working of his great power.

—Ephesians 1:17–19

≈ ≈ ≈

Trust in God's Power

Marilyn's healing from the mystery illness (pages
52–61) was a strong lesson for a young church: God
has power to heal your life. Those who prayed for
Marilyn will remember the experience forever.

That creates a confidence, not only among individuals, but in the whole church as well. The New Testament tells us that God is "able to accomplish abundantly far more than all we can ask or imagine" (Ephesians 3:20), and churches with a strong prayer life often bank on that. They might not always know *how* God is going to act, but they know he will. They live in excitement, with a sense of anticipation. When they encounter obstacles, they imagine the ways God might overcome them.

The church that prayed for Marilyn has gone on to pray for other needs, and God has mightily answered. Continued growth necessitated the construction of their own building, though they weren't always sure where the money would come from. A "culture of yes" abounds in the church. If someone has an idea for a new ministry, they explore it. No one is about to question how much God can accomplish.

It seems that Marilyn's gift of faith has been distributed throughout the congregation. Ironically, it didn't happen through her cheery demeanor or positive mental attitude. It happened when she got pushed to the brink, and others had to pray for her.

❊ ❊ ❊

Those who hope in the Lord will renew their strength. They will soar on wings like eagles; they will run and not grow weary, they will walk and not be faint.

—Isaiah 40:31 NIV

❊ ❊ ❊

Hope for the Future

The trust in God engendered by prayer creates a brighter outlook for the future. Not that people of prayer believe everything will be rosy. On the contrary, we know that struggles and challenges lie ahead. But we also know that we can talk with God about those struggles and challenges and he will lead the way through them. "Do not fear," the Lord says, "for I am with you, do not be afraid, for I am your

God; I will strengthen you, I will help you, I will uphold you with my victorious right hand" (Isaiah 41:10).

At the end of many church services, Marilyn's husband, Jeff, uses a phrase that church members hold dear: "We don't know what the future holds, but we know who holds the future." That's the hopeful attitude of people who commit themselves to prayer.

❧ ❧ ❧

Lord, we want to soar. Build us up and make us strong. Help us to use our gifts to strengthen one another and to encourage one another even in the toughest times. We don't know what the future holds, but we know that you hold the future. In Jesus' name we pray. Amen.

❧ ❧ ❧

Gathering a Church Prayer Group

~~~

How to Start One, Lead One, or Just Participate

A church singles group met every other Sunday night to study the Bible, to pray, and really just to be together. Some singles groups are all about matchmaking, but this one was more like a family. A few group members were recently divorced and needed the comfort of friends. Others were facing various upheavals in their lives—a job change, a move to a new apartment, that sort of thing.

Anywhere from four to fourteen people attended this Bible study, but it usually numbered seven or eight sitting on couches, chairs, or the floor in someone's living room. People often trickled into the meeting late, but that was fine. The first 15 minutes or so were just the gathering time. People caught up with each other over chips and drinks in the kitchen. Sometimes the leader brought his guitar and they'd all sing a few choruses. They would talk about any special outings they were planning. And then they'd dig into the Bible.

They spent three years going through the Gospel of John. Folks would joke about the slow pace—it had taken Jesus that long to *live* the Gospel of John—but it turned out to be a valuable education. Several group members were new to the faith, and they eagerly absorbed the teachings of Jesus.

Then came the prayer time. Though it started out as a routine element of the meeting, it soon became a highlight. This was when the group could connect at the heart level. Members shared the current crises of their lives, opening up to the others about their confusion, their worries, and their doubts. No pious platitudes were offered, and no one presumed to judge another member.

After the prayer requests were shared, people bowed in prayer. Anyone was welcome to speak up and voice a prayer, but there was no pressure to do so. Sometimes there was silence for a minute or two, but usually two or three would pray out loud and then the leader would launch a closing prayer.

Then, with a flurry of hugs and handshakes, the place would empty out. Maybe a few stragglers would be talking over some Scripture question or the details of the upcoming picnic, but the meeting was over.

One of the group members, Sarah, began taking notes as the prayer requests were shared. This helped her to remember what to pray for during the week, and occasionally she used her notes to ask for updates at the following meeting.

Was God actually answering the prayers of this group? Often the progress seemed very slow. Meeting after meeting, they worked through the Gospel of John, and they prayed for some situations again and again. God didn't seem to be in any hurry to answer.

But one January, Sarah pulled together the pages from the previous year and decided to review them with the group.

It was amazing. From that perspective, everyone could see that God had been working powerfully throughout the year. Suzy had needed new employment; they prayed, and she got a great new job. Deb's divorce had left her finances a mess; they prayed, and a new job helped her get back on her feet. Another divorced group member prayed for an amicable custody agreement for his daughter; he got it. Health concerns and living rearrangements and family needs had been addressed. Many had requested prayers for friends going through tough times. As they reviewed the situations they had prayed for, they were stunned and delighted by the outcomes. Of course there were ongoing struggles, but the overwhelming sense in the room was that prayer had made a difference. They gave God thanks and praise for his answers.

When the righteous cry for help, the Lord hears, and rescues them from all their troubles.

—*Psalm 34:17*

Biblical Insights for Prayer Groups

Thousands of prayer groups around the world could tell similar stories. They meet; they pray; God answers; they grow. Sure, we're dazzled by the dramatic prayer stories, where God seems to contravene the laws of nature to answer the prayers of his people. But the beauty of this group, and thousands like it, is how ordinary the prayers are. People need healing every day. They face family crises and financial needs and job issues. Prayer groups bring people together on a regular basis to consult God about these matters. They trust him to transform these situations, and he does. This is part of the ongoing process of God's loving involvement with his people.

The Book of James describes group prayer as an integral part of church life:

Are any among you suffering? They should pray. Are any cheerful? They should sing songs of praise. Are any among you sick? They should call for the elders of the church and have them pray over them, anointing them with oil in the name of the Lord. The prayer of faith will save the sick, and the Lord will raise them up; and anyone who has committed sins will be forgiven. Therefore confess your sins to one another, and pray for one another, so that you may be healed. The prayer of the righteous is powerful and effective.

—James 5:13–16

Notice the range of activity in this text. James speaks of a church where people are suffering, or cheerful, or sick, or sinful. That's us, isn't it? We struggle physically and spiritually. We suffer from the actions of others and from our own actions. And sometimes we're cheerful. When we gather, we pray for relief and sing songs of praise.

Let's take a closer look at two elements of this description.

"Anointing them with oil." A few churches practice this today, but not many. In biblical times, anointing with oil was a symbolic act depicting the outpouring of the Holy Spirit. Old Testament prophets and kings were anointed with oil as a sign of God's empowerment for their task. By the New Testament era, oil was sometimes used with healing prayers, possibly as a way of applying the Spirit's power against any demons that might be causing the illness.

> They cast out many demons, and anointed with oil many who were sick and cured them.
> —Mark 6:13

But oil also had a medical purpose. In a time long before antibiotics, olive oil could be a healing salve for some ailments. So we might find a hint here that spiritual and physical ministry go together—pray for healing, but also get treatment.

At the very least, the anointing in James 5 is an assurance to the sick person that the power of prayer has been applied to his or her situation. In the singles Bible study described above, a member asked the others to pray that she would find the power to make a difficult decision. She had finally decided to break up with a boyfriend who was holding her back in her spiritual life. It was tough to do, but she knew it was necessary. The leader had them all circle around this woman, each placing a hand on her head, and the prayer was offered in that fashion. It was not an ordinary occurrence for that group, and the leader admitted it might seem weird. "It's not that there's any magic power flowing through our hands," he said, "but there is power in our prayers. And we want her to know that we are all supporting her with that power." Empowered by this group, she ended the relationship, and her life changed for the better.

"Confess your sins to one another." Some people believe that you should go to church to show how holy you are. But you don't go to a restaurant to show how full you are! You go because you need what's there. Christians go to church because we need to meet with God. We gather with other believers because Jesus has promised to be with us in such gatherings. We need what he gives us—grace, truth, hope, and forgiveness. Especially forgiveness.

Prayer groups can be beautiful environments for spiritual growth. Christians can develop a deeper intimacy with one another in those small gatherings. Praying for one another, we can connect heart to heart. But you'll never get past the surface if you don't confess your sins. We are all struggling, seeking to know God better, but frustrated with our own failures. Prayer groups are not the place for posturing, posing, or pretending. Jesus scolded the "hypocrites" who prayed in public for everyone to see, parading their own righteousness. The word *hypocrite* was the term for an actor in the Greek theater, one who wore a mask. No, wearing a mask is not appropriate in God's kingdom, and it won't help your prayer group either. Jesus congratulated the poor in spirit, the mourners, the meek, those who knew their need for God's righteousness. These folks are well aware of their spiritual shortcomings, which they freely confess to one another.

Practically speaking, you might not need to hear all about the impure thoughts George had last week or all the details of Sally's road rage. But why not? A prayer group can be a laboratory for spiritual growth. Church prayer groups should be marked by honesty, humility, and mercy. We ask God to forgive our trespasses, even as we extend forgiveness to trespassers.

~~~

When thou prayest, rather let thy heart be without words than thy words without heart. Prayer will make a man cease from sin, or sin will entice a man to cease from prayer.

—*John Bunyan*

~~~

How to Start a Church Prayer Group

You might have several small groups in your church already actively involved in prayer, but maybe not. And if you are being nudged by the Holy Spirit to get one started, you'd better do it. Here are some basic preparations to think about.

But first, a word about definitions. The singles Bible study described at the beginning of this chapter was not really called a "prayer group," but prayer became a crucial part of its activity. That might be true for some small groups in your church, too. In some cases, however, people feel the need to focus exclusively on prayer, so they form a group just for that purpose. Either way is fine. For a small group that prays or a small group formed for the purpose of prayer—the distinction doesn't matter much— most of the following guidelines will apply.

Sanction. Every church has its own way of doing things. How will you get official approval to start a group? Talk to the pastor? Go before the board? See some other staff person? Or just do it and apologize later, if necessary?

Be aware of unofficial factors, too. Some churches have someone who's considered the "prayer person" because he or she once organized a prayer meeting

30 years ago. Touch base with such people, but don't let them hold you back.

Staff. If you're looking to start a group of six to twelve people, you might want an assistant leader. (Or perhaps you just want to get it started and let someone else lead.) An assistant can fill in if the leader is absent, but can also aid in administrative tasks like making phone calls. It's always good to have two people leading a small group.

If you want to meet in a home, you might also be looking for a host. (Even if you're meeting in the church building, a "host" might prepare the space, setting up chairs, checking the temperature, and providing refreshments.) This "staff" of one or two teammates will help you plan, publicize, and lead the prayer group.

Style. Decide what kind of group it will be. Is it for anyone in the church, or a certain age group, or just men or women? How will you spend your time together? Will there be Bible study, prayer, or both? Any singing? How long do you need for these activities—30 minutes? An hour? Two? How will the prayer time work? How open or closed will the group be? What sort of privacy issues do you need to talk about? Talk with your teammates or other advisors about the possibilities.

Schedule. Obviously you'll need to decide on a schedule. When will you meet, and how often? It's tempting to try to get people together and have the group decide, but that can be chaotic. It's probably better to make the decisions with a select few and then adjust the schedule later if the need arises.

> Likewise the Spirit helps us in our weakness; for we do not know how to pray as we ought, but that very Spirit intercedes with sighs too deep for words. And God, who searches the heart, knows what is the mind of the Spirit, because the Spirit intercedes for the saints according to the will of God.
> —Romans 8:26–27

Sell. Once you've made the decisions, you need to publicize the group. Be very clear about when and where you're meeting, and how long the meeting will last. Make sure that your invitees know they're invited. If everyone is welcome, say so.

Most churches have established ways of communicating: announcements from the pulpit, the church bulletin, perhaps a newsletter. Over time, these ordinary methods may lose their effectiveness. Instead of launching a blanket invitation, try calling people personally or talking with them face to face. People might easily ignore a generic announcement, but a personal request carries much more meaning.

~~~

How to Lead a Church Prayer Group

Once you've started the group, then what? There are lots of books and seminars that can tell you how to lead a small group, but here are some techniques to help you lead a prayer group, or any small group *at prayer.*

Consider your model. Many people, even experienced believers, feel uncomfortable praying in public, so you need to be confident in the nuts and bolts of group prayer. Decide on a format, and let everyone know what to expect. Of course there's no "right way" or "wrong way" to do group prayer, but here are a few options for you to consider.

The Anyone Can Pray Model

Share. Anyone may pray aloud. A designated closer.

Start the prayer time by asking for prayer requests. As the leader you might want to prime the pump by mentioning a need of your own, or perhaps a churchwide concern. Be sure to welcome positive matters of praise and thanks as well as items of need. As others share their requests, you might need to clarify some points or sum up. (Summing up can also be a way to get a talkative person to finish.)

When all requests have been aired, go to prayer. If there's anyone new in the group, or if you're just starting out, take a moment to explain the process. Anyone who wants to share a prayer may do so. One leader, wanting to avoid lengthy discourses, often says, "If you want to pray a few sentences out loud, that's great, but no one has to. When you've all had a chance, I'll close."

You may designate another "closer" for the prayer time, or do it yourself. This gives everyone the assurance that there will be an endpoint to this prayer time. It also gives you the chance to make sure all requests have been prayed for.

The Immediate Prayer Model

As a request is shared, the group takes time to pray for it right away.

It's not as if God suddenly arrives when you bow to pray. He's there with you as you share your needs. So why not immediately offer a prayer for each request as it is made?

After a request is voiced, the leader says, "Who would like to pray about that right now?" If someone volunteers, that person offers a short prayer about that request. When that prayer is finished, the leader asks for any other requests. When all requests have been shared and prayed for, the leader closes with a final prayer or benediction.

The Sentence Prayer Model
The emphasis is on very short prayers.

You can enhance either of the previous models by emphasizing the value of "sentence prayers." There's nothing wrong with longer prayers, but this conversational style encourages energetic participation from the group. Encourage the group to voice their agreement with the person praying or to add a new thought or concern one sentence at a time. Overlapping is nothing to worry about. As the group goes through the various requests, three or four or more people might have sentences to add to each request.

The Guided Prayer Model
A leader goes slowly through a scripted prayer, allowing the group to fill in details.

Liturgical churches might enjoy this model, which can breathe new meaning into rote prayers. Take the

Lord's Prayer, for instance. It's a great outline for your personal prayer life, but also for groups. As the leader, you could recite that prayer sentence by sentence, inviting your group to add (either vocally or in their hearts) the specifics of *why* they want to hallow the Lord's name, *how* they seek to do his will, *what* "daily bread" they need right now, *what* they need forgiveness for, and *which* temptations and evils they need deliverance from.

Set a tone. As the leader, you will set a tone for the people's prayer. Do you want the prayer to be informal or formal? Chances are, the group will follow your lead. Do you want the group to develop spiritual intimacy or keep things on the surface? The way you ask for prayer requests will affect that, as well as the way you pray.

Pay attention to comfort zones. For some people, the most terrifying thing they can imagine is praying in public. Be aware of that, and try not to put any pressure on those folks to pray out loud. Avoid situations where you "go around the circle" with everyone praying. It sounds like a good plan, but it will strike terror into some hearts.

Comfort zones also emerge when people are sharing personal prayer requests. Some group members might be vague because they want to be vague. Don't prod for more information if they don't seem comfortable divulging it.

Manage silence wisely. Some people hate silence, and they try to fill it whenever they can. But silence can also be a growing time. In prayer, silence might mean that a dozen hearts are having quality time with God. Yet silence can also put people to sleep.

As the leader, it's up to you to manage the silence. If group members trust that you know how long is too long, they will relax more within the silence. Don't leave them wondering if this silent prayer will last through next Wednesday.

Explain and observe rules of privacy. You might assume that it goes without saying: *What is said here stays here.* But you have to say it. Again and again. Church prayer groups can be hotbeds for gossip—all out of legitimate "Christian concern," of course. If you want people to share their struggles, you have to create a safety zone. Everyone has to know the rules.

Some groups go so far as to sign a contract committing them to privacy. That's not a bad idea. In any case, it needs to be an explicit agreement among group members.

~ ~ ~

Very truly, I tell you, the one who believes in me will also do the works that I do and, in fact, will do greater works than these, because I am going to the Father.

—John 14:12

~ ~ ~

How to Participate in a Church Prayer Group

What if you're not leading a prayer group, but are a member of the group? You have some responsibilities as well.

Be there. The connections formed within a prayer group strengthen with each meeting, as long as the

others know that they're going to see you there.
Make it a priority to attend the meetings. That's a
blessing for you and for the others.

Accept other group members as they are. Some of
the people you pray with might rub you the wrong
way. They might pray in an inappropriate way, or
they might hold some questionable beliefs. A prayer
group is not the place for judging, but for joining
together before the throne of grace.

Open up. Be yourself, warts and all. You don't need
to impress anyone, especially God. Be willing to
confess your sins in this group.

Look for prayer requests and answers. As you begin
to see the power of God responding to your group's
prayers, you'll start seeing prayer requests all over
the place. Every problem in your life, in your church,
and in your community will be fodder for prayer.
Bring those prayers to God in faith, and then see
what God does.

Keep it short and sweet. Say what you need to say in
the group, but don't preach any sermons. As you

share prayer requests, and as you pray, consider t...
others in the group. Perhaps someone else needs
more time to speak, so don't hog it all for yourself.

Hold your tongue outside the group. The privacy of
a prayer group is really a sacred trust. Do all you can
to maintain it. Fight the urge to gossip about things
shared in the group.

∼ ∼ ∼

Prayer Is the Soul's Sincere Desire

Prayer is the soul's sincere desire,
Unuttered or expressed,
The motion of a hidden fire
That trembles in the breast.

Prayer is the burden of a sigh
The falling of a tear,
The upward glancing of an eye,
When none but God is near....

Prayer is the contrite sinner's voice,
Returning from his ways;

While angels in their songs rejoice,
And cry, "Behold he prays!"

Prayer is the Christian's vital breath,
The Christian's native air,
His watchword at the gates of death;
He enters heaven with prayer.

O Thou, by whom we come to God,
The Life, the Truth, the Way;
The path of prayer thyself hast trod:
Lord, teach us how to pray!
                                    —James Montgomery

How to Revive a
Church Prayer Group

What if your church has a prayer group, but it's
lacking the excitement it once had? Maybe you're in
such a group right now, going through the motions
without any real power. That's a tough situation, but
there are some things you can do.

Pray about it. It's that simple—if you want to get your church jazzed about prayer, start by praying. Maybe pray with a few others who share your desires. *Voila!* You've got a prayer group.

Check your ego. Be careful that you're not just dissatisfied because people aren't praying *your way*. Ask God for an extra shot of humility before you try to change everything.

Reevaluate the needs of the group. Here's what often happens with church groups: *They forget why they started.* They keep meeting because they like to get together, but they have long since left behind their original agenda. These groups are still meeting needs, just not the needs they first planned to meet. Prayer groups can become social groups, and there's nothing wrong with social groups—but you still need a prayer group. So maybe you want to refocus the purpose of the existing group, clearing the way for a new prayer group to form.

Divide and grow. Can you start one or more additional prayer groups in the church? Maybe these could target different age groups, or just meet at different times.

Invite new people. An influx of new blood can sometimes revitalize a tired group. You don't need to take over leadership of the group—the energetic participation of new people praying will change things.

Give a pep talk. Sometimes people need to be reminded about the great privilege we have in prayer. The eternal God wants to hear from us! Maybe you can communicate this beautiful truth in an official or unofficial way that gives people a new perspective.

Any church group can become a prayer group. Chances are, your trustees, your Christian Education committee, and your stewardship team use prayer as punctuation. "Let's close in a word of prayer." Why not open up some of those meetings to more meaningful prayer? Could the trustees spend, say, 15 minutes praying that the church building would be used powerfully for the work of God? Could the Christian Education committee pray together for each student in the Sunday school classes, or for each teacher? Could these committees learn to share their personal needs and church needs and bring them to the Lord together? You don't want to keep them from doing the work they have to do, but the most important matter in the church is its relationship with God, and prayer is a great way to strengthen that relationship.

Lord, give us the wisdom and discipline we need to pray with this group regularly. Energize us. Knit us together in your love. Give us the courage to confess our sins to one another and to be honest in our dealings. We do this all in your wonderful name. Amen.

Praying with Two or Three Friends

The Power of Prayer Partnerships

Ami had struggled with anxiety as long as she could remember. Sometimes she would have panic attacks that landed her in the emergency room, gasping for breath.

These occasional episodes marked her childhood, and they continued even after she got married and had two children. Now her anxiety included them. She couldn't shake the notion that she would come down with some fatal illness, leaving her husband and children to fend for themselves. Any ache or sniffle seemed to bring on these morbid thoughts. And every time she had to attend a funeral, she felt certain that the next one would be for her.

It so happened that a good friend of hers had the same problem. Both had recently lost loved ones and, as they commiserated, they realized that they shared more than grief. Both were haunted by fear and anxiety. They compared notes about how this was affecting their families. Since both were Christians, they also worried that their anxiety displayed a lack of faith in God's care and provision.

They decided to get together every weekday morning at 5 A.M. for an hour of prayer and Scripture reading. Maybe this would begin to free them from the bonds of their panic and anxiety. As Ami tells it, "We poured our hearts out to God in a way that only two best friends can do. Sometimes we fasted for a day or a meal. We cried and laughed with God as he revealed the root cause of our fear and how it all stemmed from not being able to trust."

They did this for about a year, and amazing things started to happen in their lives. Through prayer, they were seeing areas of their character that needed to be strengthened. There were also some deep childhood wounds that needed healing—"lancing," Ami calls it. Long-hidden pain came flooding out, and that was difficult to confront, but God was binding up their broken hearts. "That year of prayer transformed us," Ami says, "creating a passion in our lives for prayer and the vulnerability that only comes in communion with others praying before a loving Father. We will never be the same again."

When Jesus promised to be there whenever "two or three" gather in his name, he meant it. It doesn't take an organized church meeting, a leader, or even an agenda. It just takes the prayers of two or three people.

Prayers are answered in such gatherings, but there's far more involved. Jesus is present in all his healing power. Ami and her friend certainly felt that, as their times of prayer provided far more therapy than a doctor ever could. These two friends were knit together in Christian love, and both were brought back to wholeness.

Getting Started: Choosing Your Prayer Partners

Where can you find prayer partners like that? Just about anywhere.

Start with your closest Christian friends. Are there people in your church with whom you already feel a spiritual bond? Perhaps they would agree to meet with you regularly for prayer. If you're married, maybe you and your spouse could pray together with another couple every week or two. Sometimes we take Christian friendship for granted, and in our busy lives it's easy to let these connections slip. Why not make it a point to join in prayer with one or two other believers you love and respect?

Consider some community connections. You might also find some connections outside the church, in your neighborhood, or in other organizations you belong to. If you're a stay-at-home parent, could you find another parent or two in the same situation? Let the kids play together while you pray together. If you participate in a community theater, a bowling league, or a fitness class, maybe you can find a few folks willing to pray with you before or after those activities. On a more serious level, people often band together for serious community causes like neighborhood watch groups, educational groups, or political action groups. You might find that some of those people are interested in putting some prayer power behind their efforts.

Think about praying with coworkers. Most people spend as much time with their coworkers as they do with their families. Maybe some of those people would like to pray with you before or after work, or on breaks. Sometimes Christians assume that everyone else is against them. Why would anyone be interested in praying with you? You'd be surprised. While they might not agree with all the doctrines that you hold, most people do believe in God and respect prayer. If you invite them at a convenient time, and in a nonthreatening way, they might just say yes.

As it is the business of tailors to make clothes and cobblers to mend shoes, so it is the business of Christians to pray.

—Martin Luther

Mission: Possible

Missionaries always seem to have good stories of answered prayer. Why? Probably because they rely on prayer a lot, and they tend to operate in more adventurous circumstances.

A group of missionaries was working in a hospital in Congo in the mid-1900s. It was a remote area, and supplies had to be driven in by truck from Kampala, Uganda, an arduous journey of 200 miles over rough terrain.

One day, a nurse noticed they were in dire need of basic medicine—aspirin, magnesium sulfate, and penicillin. One of the missionaries had already taken the truck to Kampala to get lighting fixtures for the operating room, but they hadn't checked the medical supplies before he left. There was no way to contact him, and it might be another day before he returned. How many patients would suffer without these essential supplies?

The nurse called the staff together to pray that somehow God would meet this need.

The missionary returned later that day, and three boxes marked "Lighting Fixtures" were unloaded from the truck. With some surgeries scheduled for that afternoon, the doctor decided to open these right away, but when he reached inside the first box, he found no lighting fixtures. Instead, he found cartons of aspirin. The second box contained magnesium sulfate, and the third, of course, held penicillin.

God doesn't always answer prayers so specifically, but it's wonderful when he does. Those amazing answers to prayer reassure believers that God is interested in their needs. An event like this also captures the attention of the surrounding nonbelievers. This may be another reason that missionaries have more than their share of good stories. They often put themselves in situations where they need God's reassurance, and they are working among nonbelievers who need to see God's power at work. At the hospital in Congo, the hard-working staff was certainly buoyed by this miracle.

But you don't have to go to Congo to be a missionary. In your job, in your neighborhood, even in your home, you might be at the cutting edge of God's work in the world. If you gather with a few others to pray for his kingdom, for his will, there's no telling what might happen. By praying with your neighbors, you might get drug dealers off the corner. By praying with coworkers, you might see the company turn around to the point that no layoffs are necessary. By praying with your family, you might see your kids do better in school.

I can do all things through him who strengthens me.
        —*Philippians 4:13*

Not that prayer is a magic wand that guarantees success—you are introducing a new element into your environment: a desire to see God's will accomplished. God loves to answer prayers like that, sometimes in very specific ways. As a result your group will be affirmed in their belief, and outsiders may begin to sense that God is real.

≈ ≈ ≈

Clarifying Your Agenda

Prayer partnerships come in different forms. Early on, you should be clear on the nature of your get-togethers.

Discipling pairs. Some Christians practice "discipling," where a new believer meets with a more experienced Christian to get personal coaching on following Christ. In some Christian groups, this is known as "spiritual direction." Discipling requires a high level of motivation, brutal honesty, and deep accountability. It can achieve great results, but both partners must understand what's involved.

Accountability groups. These are similar to discipling pairs, except there's not necessarily a "coach," and there may be two to six members, each with an equal interest in answering to a group for their actions. This kind of group is especially popular with people who tend not to share personal information unless they have to. In this setup, they have to.

Support partners. Twelve-step programs promote the connection between a "sponsor" and a person trying to return to wholeness. The sponsor is someone who has been there and experienced the same kind of struggle. This is very similar to both discipling and accountability groups but is specifically connected to a support program.

Spiritual growth teams. Two or three (or more) people get together to study the Bible, discuss it, and pray together. This is the sort of thing Ami and her friend did.

Intercessory teams. Two or three church members meet specifically to pray for the needs of their church. Or community members pray together for the community. The team gathers prayer requests from the larger group and goes through them in prayer.

Casual prayer time. This might mean coworkers gathering at lunchtime or students meeting before classes to ask for God's help that day. These prayers are just as meaningful as anything else on this list, but this arrangement is less demanding. This is the entry level, a great way to pray with people who don't go to your church, or even to any church, for that matter.

Imagine that someone comes to you and says, "I'd like to get together with you every week for prayer. Would you be interested?" How would you respond? More importantly, what would you need to know before you responded?

What's expected of you? Of course you need to know what the time commitment will be, but what else? What happens if you're out of town one week? Will you have to do any preparation? If it's a person from church asking you, you might want to know if they're asking you to "disciple" them, or if they think *you* need discipling. Are they proposing some sort of accountability or support arrangement, or is it just a couple of Christians praying together?

What do they mean by "prayer"? Is Bible study included? Will it involve deep, gut-wrenching soul-searching, or will you joke around a lot? Let's say the invitation comes from someone you work with. Are they trying to convert you to their religion? Are you comfortable with any rituals that may be involved?

Anyone you ask is going to wonder these things too, so you need to be very clear with the invitation. "We just want to take five minutes before work to pray to God and ask for his help. I'm asking a couple of people from different churches. Want to join us?"

> Let all who are faithful offer prayer to you; at a time of distress, the rush of mighty waters shall not reach them.
> —Psalm 32:6

Or, "I want to take an hour a week in solid Bible study and some serious prayer. I'm wondering if you're interested in that too."

Issues in Prayer Partnerships

These groups of two or three can provide energy and spiritual growth, but they have their own set of issues to be aware of.

Find the right amount of social time. Prayer partnerships are not *just* friendships, but they *are* friendships. No doubt there were times when Ami and her prayer partner did more chatting than praying, but over the course of a year they spent lots of quality time with the Lord. And the expression of friendship is never wasted time. The Lord enjoys that kind of interaction too.

But if you find that your prayer time is more of a gabfest than it should be, talk about it. Don't scold your partner, because you share the responsibility. And it's not a bad thing that you like each other so much. Still, you should be able to discipline yourselves to stay focused on prayer or Bible study, at least for a particular period of time. Maybe you even set a timer, allowing 15 minutes to catch up with each other, but after that you get serious about prayer.

The authorities don't like your prayer time. If you're trying to squeeze in prayer time at work or school, you may sense some opposition from the powers that be. Don't make this a federal case if it doesn't have to be. Communicate with the leaders involved, being very open about what you're doing and how you're doing it.

The first book of Peter talks a lot about suffering for your faith. In one section Peter addresses slaves, assuring them that it's a credit to them if they endure punishment for doing what's right. But he adds, "If you endure when you are beaten for doing wrong, what credit is that?" (1 Peter 2:19–20). That's important for modern Christians to keep in mind, especially at their place of employment. Some Christians immediately feel persecuted whenever they receive criticism. Yet in some cases, they're not being persecuted for their faith, but because they're being offensive to others. If you're getting opposition to a prayer gathering at work or school, first try to see the other side. Is there anything about your meeting that hinders the proper operation of the company or the school? Do you have permission to use the facilities? The authorities might have legitimate concerns. See if you can address these.

Then again, some managers and administrators feel skittish about anything religious. Sure, some are vehemently antireligious, but most probably just feel uneasy. Religion is for church, they think, not for work or school. Try to alleviate their legitimate concerns.

You have disagreements over doctrine. Especially if you're getting together with someone from another church, you might encounter some doctrinal differences. While this might limit the level of spiritual intimacy you feel with that person, it doesn't have to ruin the prayer partnership. If you can agree to disagree on those matters, you can focus together on the main thing: the power of God to work his will in your lives.

If you feel the other person is trying to convert you to his or her beliefs, you might feel uncomfortable. Be honest about that. Set some boundaries: "I enjoy praying with you and I respect your position, but you have to accept that I don't agree with you. I don't want you to keep trying to convince me." If the other person won't observe those boundaries, you could dissolve the partnership. Of course, you should consider whether you make the other person uncomfortable by preaching about your beliefs.

If you've opted for a casual prayer time at work or in the community, you might find yourself praying with Jews, Muslims, Mormons, or those of other faiths. Obviously there are major differences between Christianity and these religions, even to the point of wondering whether you're praying to the same God. You might find it impossible to pray with those whose views are so different from yours, but not necessarily. Scripture tells us that God loves all of humanity, and he wants people to seek him. What better way to seek him than in prayer? Yes, you have a relationship with Jesus that they don't have, so let that relationship blossom in all its radiant authenticity. Let your light shine as you treat others with love. You can encourage yourself and others to seek God fully, asking God to make himself real to each one.

One member dominates. In a group of two or three, with no defined leader, one member often takes control. This isn't always a problem, but it can be. Talk about it candidly and lovingly. If that member will not ease up, you could dissolve the partnership and find someone else who will share the time more readily.

Then again, you might be the dominant one. Pay attention to this. You might even ask another member, "Am I talking too much? Would you prefer it if I didn't run things?"

One or more members lose interest. The smaller a group is, the more you need each member. In a group of three or four, if one member misses some meetings, it's a problem. Talk with that person, encouraging more faithfulness but also offering the option to leave the group. If the person wants to stay but can't commit to regular attendance, the rest of you will need to decide whether that's acceptable.

Don't make enemies here. People can hold grudges after being asked to leave a group. Seek God's wisdom and act with love.

Be aware that small groups usually go through cycles. After two years or so, it's natural for everyone to lose interest. Don't feel bad if that happens. Maybe it's time to dissolve this partnership and start another.

And this is my prayer, that your love may overflow more and more with knowledge and full insight to help you to determine what is best, so that in the day of Christ you may be pure and blameless, having produced the harvest of righteousness that comes through Jesus Christ for the glory and praise of God.

—*Philippians 1:9–11*

≈ ≈ ≈

Embracing Prayer

After breaking her leg in a foreign country, Nona was laid up in a hospital room five thousand miles from home, feeling very, very alone. Questions rattled through her brain. Could she trust these doctors? How well would she heal? When could she get back home? Would she need to make arrangements to miss work? Would her cats get fed? How would she arrange payment for all this?

She made a few phone calls back home, trying to sort things out, including one to her pastor's wife, who tried to console her. But still the questions were nagging her. Why did all this have to happen?

That night, she had a dream in which she felt ... *embraced.* It was a very vivid feeling. A strong presence approached her and enveloped her, and somehow she knew she would be all right. She woke up much calmer than she had been. And that calm continued through the next few days as Nona left the hospital and made the trip home.

Back home, she hobbled into the Monday Bible study that was led by the pastor's wife. Nona told the group about that dream she had, the strange feeling of being embraced, and the calm that continued.

As the pastor's wife listened, her eyes grew wide. After talking with Nona on the phone, she and her husband had joined hands and prayed for her. "You're not going to believe this," she said, "but we prayed that Jesus would come over there and give you a big hug."

It doesn't take a multitude to get an answer to prayer. "If two of you agree on earth about anything you ask," Jesus promised, "it will be done for you" (Matthew 18:19). A pastor and his wife had asked God for a tender miracle for lonely Nona. An ocean away, it happened.

~ ~ ~

> *Lord, guide me to one or two friends who*
> *can join me in prayer. Let us glorify you*
> *in our relationship. Let us seek your will*
> *in our prayers. Guide us in our time*
> *together. We pray in Jesus' name. Amen.*

Praying with Your Family

~~~

Good Habits and Beyond

Many families pray before every meal, so from an early age children learn to bow their heads, fold their hands, and close their eyes. Then Dad in his sonorous baritone, or Mom in her rich alto, thank the Lord for the food they're about to eat.

Prayer is a great habit to teach a family, but it may take children a while to really get it. They pick up traditions very well, and they can master the fine points of certain procedures. For a few years, somewhere between seven and twelve, they actually enjoy playing by the rules, and they try to get everyone else to do the same.

But of course prayer is far more than bowing, folding, and closing. At some point kids need to get beyond the form and revel in the substance. When we pray, we talk with God! If that becomes a continuing reality for your family, you will give your kids a spiritual hotline that will benefit them the rest of their lives. And as you find opportunities to pray with your children, modeling and teaching a genuine interaction with God, it will enrich your family life immeasurably.

Good Habits

Robin recently prepared an afternoon snack for her two-year-old son, Jesse. Since it wasn't a regular mealtime, she put the plate in front of him and went on to other tasks. Then she noticed he wasn't eating. "What's wrong, honey?"

Jesse pointed at his food. "Pray!" he insisted.

Even at that tender age, he knew it was important to pray before eating.

Christian families often establish two regular prayer times with children: before meals and at bedtime. Sometimes a simple prayer is memorized and used repeatedly—"God is great, God is good" or "Now I lay me down to sleep" are perennial favorites. Some families create openings in these rote prayers, thanking God for other things before meals or asking God at bedtime to bless friends and family. In addition, some observe "family devotions," a service of Bible reading and prayer, at least once a week.

These are all great habits to form. Even though parents might wonder whether any genuine prayer is going on, it's beneficial to carve out these times for connecting with God. Children learn that God is important as the giver of food and the one who blesses us night and day. Even if they don't yet know what all the words mean, they learn to set aside time to honor God.

There are some things you can do to make these habitual prayers more powerful. Maybe you're already trying these things, but if not, consider them.

Make "grace" a true thanksgiving. Like many habits, saying grace can get old fast. For a while, your family might appreciate the familiarity of a rote prayer, but when the habit becomes just a habit, if it gets to the point where you might as well be saying nursery rhymes, then it's time to mix things up.

Some families *sing* grace before meals.

Some families ask each member to say something they're thankful for. As kids get older, they make a game of it—name something you're thankful for beginning with A, beginning with B, and so on.

The important thing is to really think about what you're doing. This is the "daily bread" Jesus invited us to pray for. This food has come to us by way of the kitchen, by way of the market, by way of the farm, but ultimately God has provided it. He wants us to survive by eating it, and he wants us to enjoy it.

We read in 1 Timothy 6:17 that God "richly provides us with everything for our enjoyment." So this is a great time to thank God for all the things he provides us. You don't need to preach a Thanksgiving sermon every time you sit down for a meal, but try to encourage genuine gratitude in this special moment.

Get real at bedtime. The nightly tucking-in ritual can build your relationship with your children; it can also build their relationship with God. The key theme of most bedtime prayers is that God cares for the child and those the child holds dear. Sometimes it's important to calm the child's fears. Yes, God can protect them from the things that go bump in the night. That's the sense underlying the classic prayer, "Now I lay me down to sleep."

You don't need to talk about dying in one's sleep, but do focus on God's protection and his blessing. Some kids develop long lists of blessings they want for themselves, as if they're sending a list to Santa Claus. You might encourage them to turn their attention outward, considering how God might bless others. If they make that shift, they might start listing all the people they want God to bless. This can become a game—the more people they pray for, the longer they can stay up. But you might slow them down by asking *how* they want God to bless Grandma or Jimmy next door or Spot.

Your challenge is to keep tuning into the reality of prayer. You want to turn the habitual "God bless—God bless—God bless" into an awareness that God really does bless people in various ways.

Again, don't preach. You don't want to overwhelm your child. Maybe six nights per week you can let the rote prayer happen unimpeded, but stop and talk about it every so often. The most important thing is that your kids drift off to sleep feeling loved by you and by God. This can create an intimacy that lasts for years. Some parents are still surprised (and delighted) when their teenager calls out at bedtime, "Aren't you going to come and pray with me?"

Try dinner devotions. If you keep trying to have "family devotions" and your kids hate it, join the club. That seems to be the rule rather than the exception. It's true that some parents read Scripture with all the excitement of mold growing, but others try to be creative and *still* the kids aren't interested. What can you do?

Some parents bail out and have their kids watch an educational program. That's fine, as long as you talk about it after (or even during) the program. The whole point of family devotions is *interaction*. But here's a new idea you might look into, especially if your kids are ten or older:

"We've started having discussions around the dinner table," says Tom, a father of three teenagers. "I'll come up with some question, usually a current events thing, and we'll talk about it. Each of the kids gets a chance to give an opinion. And I usually try to bring some scriptural principles into it. Then we pray about something that comes out of our discussion."

Recently, for instance, the conversation revolved around political candidates and scandals reported from their past. Tom's question was, "Do you think it should matter what someone has done in the past?" The kids all thought it shouldn't. Then Tom asked, "When you meet someone that you want to marry, will it matter what they've done in the past?" That was a different story. They ended up praying for the people they would eventually marry.

You may find some variation on the dinner table discussion, but you'll probably discover that, when it comes to scriptural instruction, at certain ages *less is more.* That is, you'll probably see more spiritual development in your children by offering bite-size content and emphasizing application.

That brings to mind a new idea: Could prayer lead the way to more exciting family devotions? There is power in praying together, as you've been learning. Could you talk with your family about how to use that power?

With this approach, your family devotions would become sort of a prayer lab. When you get together, discuss something you want to pray for as a family. Talk about what God might want to happen in that situation. Then spend some serious time in prayer, giving each child a chance to voice their request. This isn't a laundry list—you're all praying for *one thing.* Next week you can choose a new thing to pray for. At regular intervals, review what God is doing in the situations you've prayed about. See how he's answering your prayers.

❧ ❧ ❧

You awake us to delight in your praises, for you made us for yourself, and our heart is restless, until it finds its rest in you.

—*St. Augustine*

❧ ❧ ❧

Special Occasions

A mom and dad were speaking in hushed tones about their latest crisis. Dad's company was being sold, and he wasn't sure how long he would have a job. With two kids to care for, this was a major concern. Their oldest son, age four, overheard their conversation and must have recognized the worry in their voices. He asked what they were talking about.

"Daddy's upset about his job, honey," said the mom. She didn't want to hide the matter from him, but she didn't want to go into all the details either.

The son thought for a moment about how to fix his father's problem. Then he said, "Can we pray?"

"Yes," they laughed. "We can pray." And so a little child led them.

They had been teaching him about prayer, explaining that he could talk to God when he was feeling bad about something. Already he was praying every time his best friend had the slightest sniffle. Even at that tender age, he understood the basic concept of prayer. And now he was teaching them.

Prayer habits are great, but sometimes you need to break out of those traditions with special prayers for special needs. When someone in the family falls ill or has an accident, gather together for special prayer. For special events in the church or community, pull the family together for a group blessing. Or say Junior comes home with a good report card. How special would it be to call a prayer meeting specifically to thank God for helping him?

> Beloved, I pray that all may go well with you and that you may be in good health, just as it is well with your soul.
> —3 John 2

You want to get beyond the rote habits and instill an instinct in your family. When something goes especially wrong—or especially right—who should you call? God!

❧ ❧ ❧

Ongoing Reality

Barbara was a single parent with two kids and a cat. Actually, the family had owned a succession of cats, which kept wandering away. The children were ten and seven when the latest pet, Pajamas, disappeared. They were upset, of course, but honestly Barbara wasn't. She was tired of the responsibilities of cat ownership—buying stacks of cans at the grocery, cleaning the litter box, chasing after errant felines. No, she decided. That was the last cat. They would not replace it.

The children kept begging for a new one, and Barbara tried valiantly to hold her ground. Finally, she suggested, "Let's pray about it." It wasn't just a ploy to get them to drop the matter. She knew it would take a miracle to change her mind.

So they prayed. Barbara laid the matter honestly
before the Lord. The kids wanted a new cat; she
didn't. They asked for God's guidance. But then
Barbara added a request that might have been a bit
too specific. "Father, if we are to have a cat, I am
asking you to have a kitty walk up our pathway
straight to our door."

"And, Lord," added the seven-year-old, "please make
him black."

There. The prayer was prayed. There would be no
more moaning about some neighbor with kittens
"free to a good home." It was in the Lord's hands
now. If he wanted them to have a new cat, he would
have to deliver it to their door.

About six weeks later, Barbara ran across the street
to see a neighbor. As she was knocking, she heard
her children shouting from the door of their own
house. She looked back to see a small kitten walking
up the path. With cries of delight, the kids opened
their door to let it in.

The kitty had been provided. And it was black.

≈ ≈ ≈

Jesus talked about the importance of childlike faith.
We see that beautifully illustrated here. Most of us
pray with a kind of weathered faith. We believe God
can give us what we ask for, but *will* he? We know
too much theology. That's not a bad thing. We
respect God's prerogative to do things his own way.
But when children ask for bread, they expect their
loving heavenly Father to give them bread, not
stones. Barbara's kids agreed to leave the final
decision up to God, but they had no problem
expecting a miracle to occur just as they ordered it.

Maybe God answers the prayers of children in a
more precise way because of their absolute faith.

Besides the habitual prayers at regular times and the
special prayers for special occasions, you can train
your family in the ongoing reality of prayer. Let that
childlike faith flow through your everyday life. God
is there with you as you drive to the soccer game, as
you shop for groceries, and as you watch television.
You don't need an excuse to pray, and your kids
don't either. Let them know that God loves to hear

about their challenges. There are times when you're not available, or when they'd rather not confide in you, but God is always there for them.

❧ ❧ ❧

Truly I tell you, unless you change and become like children, you will never enter the kingdom of heaven. Whoever becomes humble like this child is the greatest in the kingdom of heaven.
—*Matthew 18:3–4*

❧ ❧ ❧

What Children Need to Know About Prayer

Once when Jesus was teaching, parents brought little children for him to bless. The disciples acted as bouncers, turning them away from Jesus. When he saw that, Jesus rapidly changed the policy. "Let the little children come to me," he said. "Do not stop them; for it is to such as these that the kingdom of God belongs" (Mark 10:14).

In a world of cute child actors and collectible figurines, we have no problem asserting the value of children. But it wasn't that way in Jesus' day. Children were routinely ignored. They were investments in the future, but until they could drive a plow, they weren't considered useful. Jesus bucked that trend by declaring their eternal value in God's eyes.

It's important to teach your children how much God values them. Some simple ideas for younger children can drive the point home.

God loves children, and he wants to hear from you. Children need to know that God cares about what they say, what they need, and what they want.

It's not about saying the right words, but saying what's really in your heart. Children can be extremely methodical. They will believe that they must fold their hands precisely and say certain "magic words" in order for their prayers to work. Show them, through example and teaching, that it's not about doing everything right, but about really communicating with God.

You can talk to God about anything. Jesus said that God cares for sparrows and counts the hairs on our head. He loves hearing about anything in our lives.

Praying is a great way to show love to others. We can truly help those we love by asking God to bless them. Especially when there's little else a child can do, this is a great way to offer support.

As children grow past age nine or ten, they may be ready for some more complex ideas.

You can pray silently in your heart and mind. Prayers don't always have to be spoken—they can be thought and felt.

If God doesn't give you exactly what you ask for, he gives you something better. There will be disappointments when God doesn't fill our orders precisely, but we must trust that he's got something better in mind for us. We might not always understand it or want it, but that's what trust is all about. Like the parent who gives their kid broccoli instead of candy, God knows what's best. That's why we pray, "Thy will be done."

If you're mad at God, tell him so. An honest relationship with God may include some tiffs. If you're disappointed in him or angry with him, don't turn your back. Keep telling him how you feel. That's what Moses did. Samuel too. And Elijah, Jeremiah, Peter, Paul, and even Jesus.

❧ ❧ ❧

Build yourselves up on your most holy faith; pray in the Holy Spirit; keep yourselves in the love of God; look forward to the mercy of our Lord Jesus Christ that leads to eternal life.
—Jude 20–21

❧ ❧ ❧

Adult Families

So far this chapter has assumed that the family you pray with includes children. That's not always the case. There are couples without children and couples whose children have grown up already. There are also many other sorts of families living together:

cousins and siblings and grandparents and old friends and new friends. Any way you define "family," you can make prayer a part of it. Here are a few issues that some childless families might consider.

How do you start? Many couples don't make prayer a part of their lives together until they have kids. They may pray privately, and they plan to teach their kids good prayer habits, but it just seems too *religious* to suggest that the two of them pray together. Neither one wants to sound weird. And who knows what the other might think?

It's a conversation worth having. Prayer has value in a family even if there are no kids, even if there is no trouble. It's a way of connecting with God as a team, and tapping into the "two or three" power that Jesus promised.

So take a chance and suggest it. You might start with a simple prayer habit like saying grace before dinner. And you could even begin with a rote prayer like "God is great," but try to grow into more personal prayers.

Who leads? Here's a problem that bothers many couples. The wife is more spiritually minded than the husband, so she wants to start praying with him, and he really doesn't care. But the wife also wants the husband to be the spiritual head of the home, so she won't take the initiative to make that happen. She waits for him to suggest that they pray together, and he never does. She nudges and cajoles, and maybe he finally agrees, but he has no idea how to lead a prayer. He feels uncomfortable, so he doesn't want to do it, and the prayer that was supposed to knit them together is tearing them apart.

Sound familiar? Then talk openly about it. Drop the innuendo and say what you want. Perhaps you can agree to a division of labor that matches your gifts.

Different families have different power structures and different views of leadership in the home, but the point is always this: If you want to pray together, don't wait for someone else to do it. Step up and make it happen. If your spouse or other adult family members aren't interested, you can't force them, but you can at least bring it up.

What prayer habits can keep you on track? Grace before meals is a great way to start. Some couples also pray together before bedtime. That can be a great opportunity to clear the air each night, so you "do not let the sun go down on your anger" (Ephesians 4:26). Larger households might have a weekly house meeting to talk and pray together as a group.

You are never weary of doing us good, O Lord. Let us never be weary of doing you service.

—John Wesley

Heads or Tails?

Early in their marriage, Keith and Gwen moved to a new area and started looking for a church to attend. After visiting nearly every church in town, they narrowed it down to two possibilities. Neither one was a clear favorite. It was a toss-up . . . literally.

That's right. After praying about it, they flipped a coin. They figured God was as much in control of that coin as anything else. They also asked God to keep guiding them, to make it clear whether the winning church was indeed the church for them.

It wasn't. Attending that church over the next month, they saw a number of things that troubled them, which prompted some great discussions between the two of them about what they believed.

Meanwhile, they were visited by a Sunday school teacher from the church that lost the coin toss. In that conversation, they realized this was the church where they really belonged, so they transferred, and they stayed for quite some time.

So what happened? Did God fumble the coin toss? Not at all. Were Keith and Gwen out of line in tossing the coin to begin with? No. We see here a couple of Christians who worked together to determine what God wanted for them. They prayed together and talked together throughout the process. Without their month in the "wrong" church, they might never have had some important conversations. Their experience gave them confidence that God was truly leading them to the church where they ultimately landed. And in this dynamic process, they grew in their relationship with each other, and with God.

~ ~ ~

Lord, we want this family to be a lighthouse, shining in this community for you. We want to make prayer an essential part of our life together. We want to keep meeting with you for guidance, for assurance, and for instruction. May our love mirror your love. In your holy name, Amen.

~ ~ ~

Prayer Rituals

Rote or Riches?

James always wanted to have a daily prayer time, but he never quite got in the groove. Something always came up. He might succeed for a few days, taking 15 minutes in the morning or right before bed, but it was hard to stick with a schedule.

Then a new convenience store opened a few blocks away, and James found himself walking there just about every evening. On one of those walks, he decided to pray for a few friends. It felt pretty good to get some daily exercise while using the same time to exercise his privilege to spend time with God. He tried it again the next day, and the next. Before long, he had established his own prayer ritual. Over time, his prayer list grew and transformed. Certain issues were resolved and removed from the list. Others were added. He made sure to thank God for things and ask forgiveness, but there were also many requests concerning friends and loved ones. Soon it was taking just as long to pray through the list as it took to walk to the store and back. Convenient.

One of the people on the list was a young woman at work by the name of Allison. James had overheard a religious discussion in which Allison seemed very intrigued by the idea of God's unconditional love. So James began praying, "Lord, show Allison your unconditional love."

About five years later, James was still doing his daily prayer walk. He had to admit, it was getting a little stale. Sometimes he found himself racing through his memorized prayer list without even thinking about Allison or most of the 100 other people on it. He tried to slow himself down and be more intentional about it. He didn't want to be guilty of the empty babbling Jesus warned against—but maybe that was the price of developing a good habit.

At work, Allison was asked to assist James on a project, and she was doing quite well. So well, in fact, that James was thinking about turning the whole project over to her. That would essentially be a promotion for her, and a little step down for him, but he thought it might be the right thing to do. But while he was still weighing this decision privately, James heard from another coworker. Apparently Allison had said some disparaging things about James. Not hateful things, just demeaning, a definite show of disrespect.

James was angry as he walked to the store that evening. How could she do that? He had always treated her well, and he was even thinking of sacrificing his own standing at work for her benefit. This was the thanks he got? Treading the sidewalk toward the store, he tried to refocus his thoughts on prayer. Thanking God. Asking forgiveness for these vengeful feelings. Praying for his church, his family, his friends, and his coworkers. Name by name he went, settling into the comfortable rhythms again— and then he got to the line, "Lord, show Allison your unconditional love."

That stopped him short. Did he really mean that? Yes. In spite of everything, he still wanted Allison to experience God's love.

In that moment, God spoke to him. Not audibly, but it might as well have been shouted from heaven. James sensed God's message with stunning clarity: "*You* show her my unconditional love."

And he suddenly knew that he had to do what he felt was right: He would step aside and let her take over the project after all. Even though she had criticized him, he still needed to do this unselfish deed. That's what unconditional love was all about.

You could criticize James for racing through his prayers. His prayer walk, which started as a helpful discipline, lost some meaning over time, as James became more familiar with it. And yet, for at least a few minutes every day for five years, that prayer walk also transported James into God's presence. He wasn't digging into the meaning of everything he prayed, but every so often the meaning would pop out at him. As it did in the case of Allison.

The habitual prayer put James at the point where God could speak to him. Through repetition, the prayer for Allison was tucked away in his brain until he needed it. And suddenly it was stunningly appropriate.

≈≈≈

O Lord Jesus Christ. You are the Way, the Truth, and the Life. Do not allow us to stray from you who are the Way, nor to distrust you who are the Truth, nor to rest in any other thing but you who are the Life. Teach us by your Holy Spirit what to believe, what to do, and where we can find our rest. Amen.

—adapted from Erasmus

≈≈≈

Prayers from the Past

James developed a prayer ritual for himself, such as it was, but over the centuries Christians have created many ritual prayers that have been passed on through the generations. Today, some find these prayers very helpful. They can unite groups and empower individuals. As Romans 8:26 puts it, "We do not know how to pray as we ought." When you don't know what words to use, you could borrow some well-worded prayers from traditional sources. Sure, there is always the danger that it could result in empty babbling—or it could be a very meaningful expression of your heart to God. It depends on what you do with it.

Different Christian denominations think very differently about ritual. The Catholic and Anglican traditions use it broadly. Baptists and other "free" churches generally oppose ritual, preferring to make up their prayers on the spot. Many other churches are somewhere in between, using traditional rituals when appropriate, but finding other times for extemporaneous interaction with God. There is value on both sides of that equation. Free prayers demonstrate the immediacy of a personal connection with God, but traditional rituals connect with the rich history of the church.

Christians in the free tradition are rightly worried about "vain repetitions." However, in the Book of Revelation, John's vision began with a scene of heavenly beings saying "Holy, holy, holy is the Lord God Almighty." Not only were they repeating a key word, they were echoing a prayer that Isaiah had heard eight centuries earlier! And the repetition of key words and phrases continued. "You are worthy," they sang later. "Worthy is the Lamb." And later they intoned "Hallelujah" repeatedly, in the fashion of many Psalms.

Perhaps there is value in repeating these thoughts. Certainly God never seems to tire of hearing these words of praise. And maybe we need to keep reviewing those basic concepts so they sink into our hearts. A good editor could condense the heavenly praises of Revelation to fit on a business card, but the business of worship involves far more than concise content. We must love God with all of who we are—heart, mind, soul, and body—not just the

> Devote yourselves to prayer, keeping alert in it with thanksgiving. At the same time pray for us as well that God will open to us a door for the word, that we may declare the mystery of Christ.
> —*Colossians 4:2–3*

mind. Maybe some ritual prayers can get us past the brain and into the heart.

Here's another thing to consider: There's a time to be very personal in your prayers and a time to go with the flow. Ritual prayers go with the flow of history. We join our voices with the angels and archangels, the heavenly creatures and elders, and the many believers who have gone before us. We can do that in a church worship service, with two or three other believers, or in our own personal prayer time.

When you look at it that way, praying together means more than just joining with your current friends and prayer partners. In a way, we can pray with believers from all centuries, mixing our new words with their old ones to hail the eternal Lamb. Of course we know that dead Christians aren't really dead—they have just stepped into an eternal existence with God. They're already part of that heavenly songfest. And when we kneel in prayer, we can pray *with* them to honor God and seek his kingdom.

~ ~ ~

Prayers for Your Life

Benedictine monks developed something called the "Liturgy of the Hours," with prayers to pray at six different times of the day. Some modern believers strictly follow this pattern, using the ancient prayers of the monastery. Others adapt it to their own lives. Linda, for instance, has chosen four times a day for prayer, memorizing short prayers to offer when she drives to work, at the start of her lunch break, when she gets home from work, and just before she goes to bed. She has borrowed some of her prayers from the Benedictines and others from the *Book of Common Prayer,* editing them slightly to make them her own.

This isn't all that different from a family tradition of praying before meals and at bedtime. The key thing is that you connect with God in various ways at various times of day. You don't have to memorize ancient prayers, but they might help prompt you to dedicate your day to God in the morning, to ask for strength at noon, to thank him for his provision each evening, or to request blessings for loved ones at bedtime. And yes, you might find yourself racing through some of those prayers without thinking, but parts of them just might pop out at you when you need them.

The "Jesus Prayer" is another popular ritual with very old roots in the Eastern Orthodox tradition. "Lord Jesus Christ, Son of God, have mercy on me, a sinner." (It's sometimes shortened to "Lord, have mercy.") You might recognize that as the humble prayer of the tax collector after the Pharisee trumpeted his own virtues (Luke 18:10–13).

Of course, some people carry this prayer to extremes, repeating it over and over as if to squeeze all meaning out of it. Remember: The words won't save you. This is no *mantra* that will win you inner peace. God isn't impressed with how many times you utter this phrase. But if the simple sense of this prayer can sink into your heart, that's a good thing. If the repetition serves to continually reorient you as a servant of God seeking his mercy, then it's a vehicle for growth.

An Orthodox priest was talking to a group of evangelical students about prayer. All the while he was absentmindedly fiddling with a ring on his finger. It was an old rope ring, nothing fancy, but he kept turning it as he spoke with them. One of the students asked about that, and he explained that he had developed a habit of turning the ring as he prayed a "breath prayer"—inhaling on "Lord Jesus Christ, Son of God," and exhaling on "have mercy on me, a sinner." Even as he conversed with the students, part of his brain was going through that simple prayer, and turning the ring as he did so. "It's my way to 'pray without ceasing,'" he said.

There are other breath prayers you could use, such as "I have loved you/With an everlasting love" (Jeremiah 31:3) or "My peace/I give to you" (John 14:27). The idea is to develop an instinct of prayer that's available in all situations. Your computer probably runs several programs that are always on, waiting for you to access them. Breath prayers are sort of an "always on" program for your soul. If you're driving and someone cuts you off, you might instinctively say all sorts of things. Wouldn't it be great if you prepared yourself to yell out, "Lord have mercy on me!" in such instances?

What if you could train part of your brain to pray all the time? What if you were constantly repeating a simple prayer—"Lord, have mercy" or "Jesus loves me" or "I seek first your kingdom"—while you worked, ate, played racquetball, or chatted with friends? That's essentially what some people try to do with breath prayers.

Writing in the sixteenth century, Ignatius of Loyola taught the first Jesuits a prayer of self-examination. This *Examen,* as it's known, involves a series of questions you might ask yourself at the end of each day. Over the centuries, Christians have adapted these questions in various ways, but the essence is the same. Here's one version of that process:

Question 1: What happened today for which you are most grateful? Thank God for these things.

Question 2: What happened today for which you are least grateful? Work through these things with the

Lord. They might include sins you should ask forgiveness for or challenges you need to learn from.

Question 3: What do you expect to happen tomorrow? Offer yourself to God, dedicating the next day to him.

This simple procedure serves as a valuable daily recalibration. Are you on track with God? Are you learning, are you growing, are you stepping forward in your relationship with him? If you're so inclined, you could look up the original *Examen* and see all that Ignatius did with it. He even developed a kind of self-help book for overcoming temptation, using daily checkpoints like these.

Taken together, the Liturgy of the Hours, the Jesus Prayer or other breath prayers, and the *Examen* have been used by thousands, even millions of Christians through the ages. With these methods, prayer becomes not only a conversation with God (as valuable as that is), but an intentional process of spiritual growth. By praying together with all those who have preceded us, we can experience that soul-growing power as well.

Hebrews 12:1 says we are surrounded by a "great cloud of witnesses," and therefore we should "run with perseverance the race that is set before us." What's that about? What is a cloud of witnesses? Well, the previous chapter is sort of a Hall of Fame, or perhaps a Hall of Faith, recounting the faith of Abraham, Joseph, Moses, and other Old Testament heroes. That's the cloud of witnesses looking on as we grow in our own faith. As we access some of the ancient traditions, we can join our prayers with theirs to praise and please our Lord.

Faith is the assurance of things hoped for, the conviction of things not seen. Indeed, by faith our ancestors received approval. By faith we understand that the worlds were prepared by the word of God, so that what is seen was made from things that are not visible.
—*Hebrews 11:1–3*

~ ~ ~

Mad About You

For several weeks, as she attended her church, Ann was upset. She and her husband, Jack, had been serving in positions of leadership in the church, and they had worked hard. Many church people had expressed appreciation for their efforts, but apparently the pastor felt threatened. He arranged for Ann and Jack to be dismissed from their positions.

They were stunned. They had always been team players, looking to serve humbly. Where was this coming from? They were being maligned, insulted, and mistreated. Certainly they deserved better treatment than this.

They thought about leaving the church, but how could they? It was their home. They had deep relationships with many of the people there. Some friends suggested that they stage a big protest to get their positions back, but Ann and Jack wouldn't hear of it. They didn't want to divide the church. Yet there was a division—it was impossible for them to look the pastor in the eye. And sitting in the congregation listening to him preach was extremely difficult. Ann, especially, was seething with anger. But what could she do about it?

Somewhere along the line, she had been given a prayer ring, a simple metal piece with some indentations and bumps. Unable to focus on anything else, she focused on this ring, running a finger along those little bumps and creating a new breath prayer, "Lord, I forgive. Lord, I forgive. Lord, I forgive."

Did she feel like forgiving? No way. Her emotions were raging in protest of the treatment she and Jack had received. But this prayer was an act of the will. She was choosing the way of Christ—the way of forgiveness. She knew that she was a sinner in need of forgiveness, so she needed to extend it to others, in spite of her feelings. "Lord, I forgive. Lord, I forgive. Lord, I forgive."

Was this hypocritical? Was she denying her true feelings? Was she pretending to be holier than she really was? Those things might be true in some situations, but not in this one. She knew very well that she felt anger, and she was in a mighty struggle with it. Her prayer was not a denial of her true feelings, but a decision to put those feelings in their place. She was trying to "take every thought captive to obey Christ" (2 Corinthians 10:5), deciding that her desire to follow Christ in the way of forgiveness would take precedence over her vengeful emotions.

It was a strategy she had learned from ancient Orthodox believers. Let every breath be a prayer, so even when you don't know what to say, you'll have something to offer the Lord.

Almighty God, all hearts are open to you, all desires known. We have no secrets from you. Breathe your Holy Spirit upon us and cleanse our thoughts and longings, so that we might perfectly love you. Make us worthy to magnify your holy name, through Christ our Lord, Amen.

—adapted from an ancient church prayer

High-Tech Prayer

v Methods in the rnet Age

chool when her body began its re... ...n. Sudden..., ...t stopped doing what she wanted it to do. Barbara had been active in sports and music, but no more. Multiple sclerosis was crippling her.

The next decade saw a continuing decline. Barbara lost the use of her arms and legs, and some of her internal organs were giving out. It was hard for her to breathe. By age 30 she was nearly blind.

Doctors admitted they could do nothing to halt the disease. Her only hope was prayer. Though she had long been a Christian, she hadn't been praying much lately. As her body was increasingly consumed by MS, her soul was consumed with anger. How could God let this happen to her?

But when all hope was gone, she reached out again in prayer, and she got a strange answer. *Pray for others,* the Lord seemed to be telling her. She began to do just that. When visitors came to cheer her up, she offered to pray for *them.* Though her physical deterioration went on, others began to notice her spiritual renewal.

Then a radio program told her story, inviting listeners to pray for her and to write to her. She received 450 letters over the next few weeks. People out there in radioland were lifting her up in prayer and telling her so. Two friends were sitting with her, reading some of these letters, when Barbara heard a soft voice saying, "My child, get up and walk."

Her friends didn't hear anything, so either she was losing her mind or something supernatural was taking place. She decided to test it, pushing back her bed covers and placing her foot on the floor. She stepped on it. She was standing! She stepped forward. She was walking! She met her parents in the hallway. She was moving with a freedom she hadn't enjoyed since high school.

The next day she walked into her doctor's office. At first he thought it wasn't possible, but tests confirmed the miracle. There was no sign of MS in her body. Other doctors verified it. There is no medical cure for MS; they had no way of explaining this; but the facts of the case spoke for themselves. A miracle had happened.

More than two decades later, Barbara is still living a normal, MS-free life in Virginia. And if you believe in a supernatural God who sometimes chooses to answer the prayers of his people by upending the laws of nature, then it's not too hard to accept this account. What makes it especially interesting is that Barbara had hundreds, probably thousands of

> For everything created by God is good, and nothing is to be rejected, provided it is received with thanksgiving; for it is sanctified by God's word and by prayer.
> —I Timothy 4:4–5

Christians praying for her, even though they had never met her. Barbara's story went out over the airwaves, and their prayers ascended on a different kind of airwave, and God chose to honor their requests for healing.

When Jesus said that he would be wherever two or three gathered in his name, no one could have anticipated that radio waves could one day send prayer requests throughout an entire metropolitan area, or that satellite broadcasts could unite the world in viewing the same event, or that the Internet would connect Americans with Australians, Austrians, and Argentineans as if they were next-door neighbors.

Technology has changed our definitions. When John Wesley was pioneering the small-group movement in his Methodist churches in the late 1700s, he had no idea that prayer groups would one day form in virtual chat rooms, or that cables would instantly carry the images of television evangelists farther than circuit-riding preachers could ever hope to travel, or that his brother's hymns would be digitally mixed, remixed, transmitted, and stored in computer files.

Some people expect group prayer to happen in person, with two, three, or more believers forming a circle or linking hands. But if you want to pray with someone far away, why *not* use the telephone? Or the computer?

Increasingly, Christians are "getting together" to pray over the Internet, through instant messaging chats, or with e-mail messages. That might present a challenge for some folks who aren't yet computer savvy. It's true that you won't find the warmth of a real-life prayer group online, and you can forget about the laying on of hands. You'll be laying your hands on the keyboard, pecking out your prayers for people you've never seen. But for a new generation of prayer warriors, the Internet is where things happen. *Why not* use it to connect in prayer?

❧ ❧ ❧

God, almighty and merciful, may we poor sinners do all that we know of your will, and to will always what pleases you, so that kindled by the Holy Spirit, we may follow in the footprints of your well-beloved Son, our Lord Jesus Christ. Amen.

—*St. Francis of Assisi*

❧ ❧ ❧

What's the Net Worth?

Today, every major business has a Web site, more than half of Americans have access to the World Wide Web, and people spend hours a day online. For many, sending e-mail has taken the place of writing letters. For some, it has replaced telephone conversations. Shopping, research, even dating can be done online. Who needs stores, libraries, or singles clubs when you can sit down at a computer and visit all three with the touch of a few buttons?

That's good news and bad news.

Every new medium has its pluses and minuses, and the Internet is no exception. For every legitimate business on the Web, there's a handful of con artists. For every virtual prayer chapel, there are a hundred "adult" sites. It's a mixed bag.

When you boil it all down, the Internet has two basic features that seem entirely contradictory. It is the greatest *connecting* device the world has ever seen. Within moments you can hold a conversation with people on any continent. You can find information on just about any topic. You can buy or sell just about any product.

Ironically, the Internet is also dangerously *isolating*. Generally, people step away from their friends and families and sit alone at a computer to surf the Web. PCs—personal computers—are built to be, well, *personal*. They're made for one, and so much of what's done on a computer is private. That's why so many people get into trouble chatting about or viewing things that they wouldn't consider under other circumstances—there's no one beside them to check their actions. Online, they inhabit their own little world, connecting with anyone or anything while remaining virtually anonymous. Relationships formed via the Internet might seem rapidly intimate, but they're actually quite shallow. Some marriages are shattered when a husband or wife leaves for an Internet chat partner. They assume the new partner knows them deeply, because they've dished all sorts of details in their computer chats. Sadly, the reality is quite different.

Keep these cautions in mind as you enter the world of online prayer. Great connections can be made— no doubt about it. You will be able to connect soul to soul with some wonderful Christians. Yet you must recognize that online relationships are never as deep as they seem, and be careful not to isolate yourself from real-life relationships. Real life is harder but usually healthier.

It would be foolish, however, to entirely avoid Internet prayer opportunities because of possible dangers of the medium. As long as you're smart about it, you can safely navigate the Internet and make some genuinely positive connections.

❧ ❧ ❧

E-mail Prayer Partners

The Andersons weren't very good at writing letters, and their busy schedules made it difficult to call as frequently as they wanted. Mom and Dad were in their late 60s, and their three grown children were scattered across the country. They all loved getting together at Christmas, but other than that, it was tough to stay connected. Then came e-mail.

"It's like I don't have to compose a long, formal letter," says one of the Anderson siblings. "I can just zap over the simplest thought any time I want." Besides that, any one of them can send off a message late at night that their folks can read the next morning. E-mail has enabled them to reconnect in meaningful ways. Via e-mail, they've planned their Christmas gatherings and even arranged to take some vacations together. One of the kids is working on a research project with the parents. And lately they've been sending digital pictures to one another.

The same story could be told about many families and friends. The great connectivity of the Internet has its blessings. Relationships can be built, strengthened, and maintained through cyber-correspondence.

So why not use it to develop prayer partnerships?

Be intentional about prayer. You may already be e-mailing back and forth with some Christian friends. But have you ever shared prayer requests? Have you ever typed out the prayer you're praying for that friend and sent it along? Have you ever connected in an instant message chat with someone and prayed together?

Those things won't just happen. You'll need to decide to do them. Send an e-mail explaining the kind of prayer partnership you'd like. Maybe every week you each send the other whatever prayer requests you have. Or you can arrange some time during the week for a prayer chat. (The phone can be used too.) Maybe you just start sending e-mail notes to the people you're praying for: "Here's what I'm praying for you . . . Lord, bless this precious friend in these ways..." If that sounds weird to you, check out Ephesians 1:17 or Philippians 1:9–11. The apostle Paul said the same thing, only on papyrus.

❧ ❧ ❧

I pray that the God of our Lord Jesus Christ, the Father of glory, may give you a spirit of wisdom and revelation as you come to know him.

—Ephesians 1:17

❧ ❧ ❧

Follow up on answers. Some folks get as far as sharing prayer requests but never check back to see how things are going. Perhaps you could even keep a computer file of the prayer requests you receive. Depending on how organized you are, you might even create a spreadsheet listing the subject of your prayers and follow-up news. God answers prayer in all sorts of ways, so this needs to be more than a checklist. Leave room for surprises, lessons learned, and collateral blessings. But it always helps to remember what we've prayed for, so we can see God at work.

Make real-life connections. One danger of the Internet is that it entices people away from daily life by immersing them in cyberspace. The Internet works best when it's used alongside other life experiences. The Andersons found that their ongoing e-mail correspondence enhanced the time they spent together. You can create the same sort of dynamic in your online prayer partnerships.

Don't let e-mail replace personal interactions. Let both work together to keep you socially well rounded. Share your prayer requests with distant friends via e-mail, but pray for and with your local friends and neighbors as well.

❧❧❧

Give us grace, we humbly pray, to be ever willing and ready to minister to the necessities of our fellow-creatures, and to extend the blessings of your kingdom over all the world, to your praise and glory.

—*St. Augustine*

❧ ❧ ❧

Prayer-based Web Sites

If you type "prayer chat" into an Internet search engine, you will receive pages of results. (You might try some other configurations of words to fine-tune the results.) By clicking on some of those listings, you can enter various chat rooms, bulletin boards, or other Web sites—most of them focusing on prayer. On some of them, you can post your prayer requests for others to read, and you can read their requests for prayer. On others, you can enter a live "prayer chat," where you can share requests and prayers in real time. Still others teach about prayer. It all sounds like a foretaste of heaven, right? Well, not necessarily. You still must navigate carefully.

Don't divulge information that's too personal. The fact is, you don't know who else is visiting this Web site. Ninety-five percent might be wonderful Christian people, but the other 5 percent might not be. Predators of all sorts prowl the Internet, and Christians are known to be very trusting people. So it would be no surprise to find impostors online trying to steal your money, your identity, your reputation, your morality, your faith, or something else. As Jesus said, "Be wise as serpents and innocent as doves" (Matthew 10:16). Don't be paranoid, but don't be gullible either.

Whenever you're online, be very careful about giving any sort of financial information. But other personal information could be used against you as well. This gets tricky when you're asking for prayer for personal matters. Be protective about any identifying details, especially children's names and ages, their school, family birthdays, your town, or your employer. God knows those details; they don't have to be revealed to prayer partners you've just met.

Shrug off opposing theology. Guaranteed: You will meet people online with beliefs that are very different from yours. Respect the differences, but don't let them sway you from your own doctrines. On the other hand, you shouldn't try to change anyone else's theology either. If you can hold a well-reasoned doctrinal discussion, fine, but remember, you're there to pray. If you feel that the tone or teaching of a particular Web site is bothersome, find another. You might have to try out ten or twelve sites before you really feel at home in one.

Another characteristic of the Internet is its freedom. In many aspects, the Web is unregulated. That goes for its doctrine, too. Internet religion has no bishops or elders, no church hierarchy checking its accuracy, so you shouldn't be surprised to find a whole spectrum of beliefs represented there. Keep your spiritual balance. Check out any radically new ideas with your own spiritual leaders—your pastor or other teachers in your church.

Respond to need, but don't be overwhelmed by it.
You will also find many needy souls on the Internet, especially in the prayer sites. Your heart will be broken by the stories of those who are seeking prayer. What can you offer? Prayer, of course. Encouragement, certainly. Beyond that, there's not a lot you can do. Do *not* send money to someone you meet online, no matter how desperate they seem. (Many prayer sites have rules against such requests.) You can always urge someone to seek help from established churches and charities, and you might be

able to recommend a particular charity. Do *not* give out your phone number or address in an attempt to help the person in a more personal way. That might sound cruel, but it's just a matter of wisdom. Prayer is powerful. Let that be your main way to meet the awesome needs you'll encounter.

Follow the rules. Most chat rooms and Web sites have rules posted. Check these out as you enter, and honor them throughout your visit. One common rule is confidentiality. What's said there should stay there.

Be yourself. In the anonymity of the Internet, you might be tempted to masquerade as someone more (or less) spiritual than you really are. You might feel pressure to pray pompously or to use religious language. Just be yourself. Ultimately, you will be offering your prayers to God, who sees you exactly as you are.

> Rejoice in hope, be patient in suffering, persevere in prayer.
> —*Romans 12:12*

Don't let the Internet replace the church. With the Internet making libraries, department stores, and post offices obsolete, how long before it takes the place of the church? You can download preaching and praise music, and you can chat all day with other Christians. What else do you need?

Real connections with people. Deep relationships. Accountability. Commitment. Participation.

Internet prayer sites can provide a piece of churchlike experience, and that can be a great thing. But don't let it draw you away from a real commitment to your church. You might think you're developing deep Christian fellowship with your new online friends, but it's probably not as deep as you think. And don't underestimate the value of your weekly participation with your church.

❧ ❧ ❧

Lord, we know not what we ought to ask of you. Only you know what we need. You love us more than we know how to love ourselves. We have no other desire than to do your will.

—François Fénelon

~~~

Church Web Sites

As a youth pastor, Drew often found himself working on his computer in the afternoon, doing Internet research or e-mailing some of the staff. Then he started getting instant messages from the kids in the youth group. One, then three, then six. Sometimes there were ten or twelve students saying hi with instant messages. Occasionally someone would have a question about the youth group schedule, and once in a while there was a spiritual question. But for the most part, it was just kids hanging out. In a previous generation, kids would loiter in front of the local convenience store. Now they were sitting in front of their computers with open lines to all their buddies.

Drew began to wonder if that phenomenon could be turned into a Bible study or prayer group. Could he make himself available for Bible questions between 2 and 4 every Tuesday? Could he pray with kids online every Thursday? At this writing, those brainstorms are still in the works.

This is the cutting edge of communication, and it makes sense for churches to use every resource available to fulfill their calling. Many churches these days have Web sites, and some are beginning to harness instant messaging technology for online groups. In an age when people are very busy, when families treasure their time at home and parents find it hard to get sitters, you don't want to bring folks out to church every night of the week. Why not use the Internet for a virtual small group meeting? Why not hold your church's midweek prayer meeting online?

If you go that route, here are a few ideas:

Get technical know-how from young people. As you've probably noticed, kids know far more than adults about the latest technology. Many older adults struggle with computer basics, while twelve-year-olds have mastered complicated systems. Asking for help would be a great way to get teenagers and twenty-somethings more involved in the operations of the church. Why not let them develop a cutting-edge Internet presence for the church, complete with prayer lines so church needs get instant prayer attention?

Provide good leadership. In general, the Internet is a free-for-all. People do whatever they will. Even on some Christian prayer sites, you often find a lack of leadership. That's where a church can fill a need. An imaginative church Web site, with the proper vision, can chart a clear course for the future. You can meet a variety of needs in the congregation and community while staying true to your church's mission. So make sure your Web site has clear direction.

In many churches, the spiritual leaders are downright ignorant of technical matters. That doesn't have to be a problem. You just need to communicate well and learn from one another, leaders and techies working together to create effective ministry.

Follow up with personal care. Your church's Web presence should augment your physical ministry. Make new connections online, but whenever possible, seek to supplement that ministry in some tangible way.

❧❧❧

The Chain

One church began an e-mail prayer chain a couple of years ago. Requests are e-mailed to the coordinator, who sends them out to about 70 church members, who pray. Sometimes they hear back about the results of their prayers.

A man was facing back surgery. Later he expressed thanks to all the prayer warriors, because he knew that's what got him through.

A soldier returned safely from Iraq.

And there was prayer for a paralyzed teenager and the mother who cared for him. The outlook was bleak when the prayer request first went out, but the situation improved gradually. The boy is better than the doctors anticipated, and he's determined to do even better. His mother, once discouraged, now has a more positive outlook, not only on her son's prognosis, but in every area of her life. She related to the prayer-chain coordinator that she was "becoming a believer in prayer again."

In this new way for a new technological age, Christians are calling one another to join in the age-old practice of praying together. And it's as powerful as ever.

❧ ❧ ❧

> *Lord, we're going to keep seeking new ways to pray together. As this world creates new methods of communication, we will use them to share our needs and to unite in our praises. Help us to use every medium wisely, so that you will be honored above all. In Jesus' name, Amen.*

❧ ❧ ❧

Tapping Into the Power

Energize Your Church with Prayer

Maria remembers the prayers her youth group shared on a mission trip. They had journeyed from their New Jersey homes to upstate New York to help refurbish houses in a needy area. The kids were excited about helping others, but they also just loved being together.

In the evening, muscles sore, they gathered for a time of worship. Scripture was read, the leader spoke, songs were sung, and then it came time to pray. The leader invited them to pray out loud, but the kids seemed hesitant. They had no problem joining in when the group was singing, but to speak up personally, talking to God in front of a jury of their peers? That was scary.

Maybe it was the day of bone-bending work that quashed their resistance. Maybe they were too tired to keep their defenses up. In any case, a miracle happened that night. One teenager started to pray, but not in any pious language. She was simply letting God know how she felt. Empowered by that example, Maria launched her own prayer. She spoke freely, not editing her words, just pouring out her heart to God. Then the dam broke. One after another, the kids spoke up, thanking God and praising God, blessing God and begging for God's blessings, recounting the events of the day and asking God to be with them tomorrow.

"It was like God was there with us," Maria says, "not some distant figure walking down the street."

Now in college, Maria helps lead the same youth group, which is twice the size it was then. Several teens and leaders look back at that mission trip—at that prayer time—as a breakthrough. That's when they learned the power of praying together.

~ ~ ~

O God, make the door of this house wide enough to receive all who need human love and fellowship; narrow enough to shut out all envy, pride and strife. Make its threshold smooth enough to be no stumbling block to children, nor to straying feet, but rugged and strong enough to turn back the tempter's power. God, make the door of this house the gateway to thine eternal kingdom.

—Bishop Thomas Ken

~ ~ ~

Strangeness

You've read a number of miracle stories in this book. People pray, and amazing things happen. Yes, phenomenal moments occur when we invite the Lord into the events of our lives. Sometimes God gives us exactly what we ask for, sometimes he dazzles us with something better, and sometimes he bends his own rules of nature to do so.

Skeptics might say, "But those things just don't happen!"

We can answer, "That's why they're called *miracles.*" The word comes from the Latin for *strange.* By definition, a miracle is something that makes you wonder. The skeptic is right to say that miracles don't *ordinarily* happen, but it's irresponsible to say they *can't.* If you believe in a God who exists above and beyond nature, it's no stretch to think he might miraculously heal a disease or open a prison door or even provide a kitten for a young family.

But the power of prayer has another side, too. As we make contact with God, we can't help but be affected ourselves. When Moses met God on Mount Sinai, we're told, his face radiated light for days afterward. The same sort of thing happens to us, not outwardly shining, but inwardly. After hanging out with God, we radiate his love, his joy, his peace.

Scripture shows us both sides of the coin. Amazingly, God does want to hear what we want, and he often merges our desires with his to work miracles. But he also changes us, helping us grow and conform to the image of Christ. He challenges us, teaches us, and comforts us, all through the power of prayer.

What a friend we have in Jesus,
all our sins and griefs to bear!
What a privilege to carry
ev'rything to God in prayer!
O what peace we often forfeit,
O what needless pain we bear,
All because we do not carry
ev'rything to God in prayer.

Have we trials and temptations?
Is there trouble anywhere?
We should never be discouraged—
take it to the Lord in prayer.
Can we find a friend so faithful,
who will all our sorrows share?
Jesus knows our ev'ry weakness—
take it to the Lord in prayer.

Are we weak and heavy laden,
cumbered with a load of care?

Precious Savior, still our refuge—
take it to the Lord in prayer!
Do thy friends despise, forsake you?
Take it to the Lord in prayer!
In his arms he'll take and shield you—
you will find a solace there.

—Joseph Scriven

❦ ❦ ❦

Bearing Burdens

Dave is still talking about a men's retreat from
several years ago that featured an intense experience
of prayer. One of the men attending, a senior citizen,
had lost his wife three weeks earlier. They had been
married for half a century, so it's understandable
that this man was feeling a bit lost. Throughout that
weekend, though, there were several times of prayer,
when men clapped hands on the shoulders of other
men and stormed the portals of heaven. For the
recently widowed man, they prayed that God might
ease his deep pain. Galatians 6:2 says, "Bear one
another's burdens, and in this way you will fulfill the
law of Christ," and that's what they offered to do, to

"bear his burdens" so that he might be restored to emotional health.

The miracle that happened that weekend was nothing that will go down in history. The natural order of life was not overturned. But the burden of pain felt by one grieving man was disbursed among a dozen others. Years later, he was still thanking them: "Those prayers made such a difference in my life."

> Pray in the Spirit at all times in every prayer and supplication. To that end keep alert and always persevere in supplication for all the saints.
> —Ephesians 6:18

When we pray, our prayers knit us together. We find our place together before Almighty God, longing for his will to be done. Sometimes God uses us to answer one another's prayers, and sometimes the group experience is enough to challenge, teach, or comfort us.

Power in Prayer

Are you looking for power in your life? In your family interaction? In your church? There is power in prayer. You can tap into that power by praying individually, but you elevate that power to a new dimension when you rally others to pray with you.

Many people feel frustrated because they keep going to church and nothing seems to happen. Church is as it always was. They long for some act of God to shake the rafters. Well, maybe the answer can be found in prayer.

Gather a few friends together to pray for the church. Present the needs of church members before the Lord. Seek his will, his kingdom, and take time to listen for his direction. Your little group might grow to a dozen or more. Or maybe it will always be two or three believers, summoning the power of God to infuse the work of your church. That power will change *you* as well.

Many people these days feel angry when they look at trends in the culture. It seems the world is going downhill fast, and we are powerless to do anything about it. Well, we're not powerless—we can pray. The power of prayer will change things in surprising ways. Oh, there will always be those who flout God's commands, but even in the midst of flagrant disobedience, God's power can protect and inspire.

So why not suggest to some neighbors, some friends, or some coworkers that you gather once a month to pray in a nonsectarian way for the needs of the nation and the world? You might be surprised at what happens.

Many people today feel desperate when they think about their families. Their kids are becoming difficult, and maybe their marriage is too. They long for some kind of divine power to sweep in and do what they cannot do, at least to hold things together. Maybe even to rekindle love.

Start praying together. There's no need for a big worship service. Don't preach. Just gather for ten minutes and give each family member a chance to talk with God out loud. Let everyone else in your family see your honest interaction with your heavenly Father, and encourage them to speak honestly with God as well. No one has to put on an act. You're not trying to impress God or anyone else. Just lay your soul before God with all your faults and foibles, and beg him to make things better.

Under the Headlines

Perhaps you saw the headlines a few years ago. Two young women, working for a Christian relief agency, were arrested in Afghanistan. Reportedly they had shared a book and film about Jesus with an Afghan family that had expressed interest. According to the Taliban leadership, such proselytizing was illegal, deserving the death penalty.

At first these two women, just a few years out of college, were kept in a 10×10-foot cell under miserable conditions. They saw other prisoners brutally beaten. Cut off from any contact with their attorney or their homes, they faced a bleak future. About two months into their detainment, the United States began bombing Taliban terrorist sites in Afghanistan. It looked as if their release would never be negotiated.

But there was a major force flying under the headlines. Both young women belonged to a dynamic church in Waco, Texas. The church had supported their mission, and now they were praying nonstop for their release. A Web site was started to mobilize the prayers of the nation. The pastor asked God for a miracle like the release of Peter from prison in Acts 12.

Meanwhile, the women were hearing the bombs fall around them. They *felt* the bombs shake the prison walls. At one point, the Taliban guards herded them out into a van, fleeing the area.

The next hours were chaos. After spending the night in a makeshift prison, the young women saw the door flung open. Their guards were gone, and an opposition commander was saying, "You're free!

You're free!" Out in the open, they were in the middle of a conflict. They had to set their head coverings on fire to flag down a rescue helicopter, but soon they were on their way to safety.

Gratefully, they returned to the church and the nation that had won their release with their powerful prayers.

~ ~ ~

The power of prayer is always on, always available to you. To tap into this amazing resource, all you have to do is pray. Better yet, grab another two or three believers and pray together.

~ ~ ~

Lord, empower us to pray courageously and effectively. Fill our hearts with a desire to seek your kingdom. We honor you and love you. Bless our efforts to gather in prayer, and we will give you all the glory, in Jesus' name. Amen.